© Copyright 2017 b
rights reserved.

Legal Notice:

The book is copyright protected. This is only for personal use. You cannot amend, distribute, sell, use, quote or paraphrase any part or the content within this book without the consent of the author.

Disclaimer Notice:

Please note the information contained within this document is for educational and entertainment purposes only. Every attempt has been made to provide accurate, up to date and reliable complete information. No warranties of any kind are expressed or implied. Readers acknowledge that the author is not engaging in the rendering of legal, financial, medical or professional advice. The content of this book has been derived from various sources. Please consult a licensed professional before attempting any techniques outlined in this book.

By reading this document, the reader agrees that under no circumstances are is the author responsible for any loses, direct or indirect, which are incurred as a result the use of information contained within this document, including, but not limited to, —errors, omissions, or inaccuracies.

Introduction...

Vegetarian vs. Vegan... 8

3 Types of Vegetarians: Which One Are You?................... 9

Health Benefits of a Vegetarian Diet............................... 9

Drawbacks to a Plant-Based Diet................................. 11

What You Can Expect in this Cookbook......................... 11

Instant Pot: What it is and Why You Need One............. 13

Appetizers & Snacks... 15

    Easy Cheesy Beer Dip...................................... 15

    Eggplant Bruschetta... 16

    Fried Garlic Potato Ravioli................................. 17

    Ginger Tofu Pot Stickers................................... 19

    Greek Feta Dip.. 20

    Kale & Ginger Spring Rolls................................ 21

    Mini Black Bean Burgers................................... 23

    Roasted Garlic Hummus................................... 25

    Spicy Black Bean Dip....................................... 26

    Spicy Tofu Lettuce Wraps................................. 27

    Spinach & Asiago Dip...................................... 29

    Sweet Potato Quesadillas................................. 30

Sweet & Spicy Cheesy Corn Dip.. 31

Veggie Dumplings.. 32

Breakfast Recipes..33

Banana Chocolate Rice Pudding... 33

Breakfast Bread Pudding...34

Cheesy Tater Tot Casserole... 36

Fall French Toast Casserole... 37

Mediterranean Baked Eggs.. 39

Not So Scotch Eggs...40

Peaches 'N Cream Coffee Cake... 42

Peach Compote.. 44

South of the Border Baked Eggs.. 45

Spiced Apple Quinoa...46

Spinach & Quinoa Power Up... 47

Steel Cut Carrot Cake... 48

Super Scrambled Breakfast Tacos.. 49

Tofu & Pepper Breakfast Burrito.. 51

Zucchini Breakfast Quiche... 52

Main Dishes.. 53

Asian Style Sautéed Eggplant... 53

Cannellini in Tomato Sauce..................................54

Cauliflower Coconut Curry....................................56

Easy Saag Tofu...57

Faux Chow Mein..59

Gumbo...60

Lentil Chili..63

Lightning Lo Mein..64

Orange Tofu & Rice..65

Peanut Sauced Tofu...66

Poblano & Zucchini Enchiladas............................67

Quinoa Enchiladas...69

Slow Cooked Stroganoff..71

Spaghetti & Lentil Meatballs.................................72

Stuffed Red Peppers..74

Super Simple Mac 'N Cheese................................75

Sweet Potato Pasta with Cashew Sauce..............76

Tofu Curry..77

Tomato & Spinach Frittata....................................78

Winter Squash Lasagna..79

Side Dishes...81

Apple Sage Stuffing 81

Austrian Stewed Cabbage 82

Basic Risotto 83

Brussel Sprouts with Parmesan 84

Cheesy Broccoli Casserole 85

Creamy BBQ Cauliflower 86

Easy Cheesy Cauliflower 87

Easy Corn Soufflé 88

Fried Cabbage & Rice 89

Italian Red Potatoes 91

Maple Glazed Carrots 92

Sweet Potato & Apple Casserole 93

Sweet Potato Risotto 94

Zucchini Fritters with Garlic Dipping Sauce 95

Soups & Stews 97

African Spicy Peanut Stew 97

Asparagus Lemon Bisque 99

Autumn Veggie Stew 100

Carrot Cashew Bisque 101

Cheesy Spinach Bisque 102

Creamy Cauliflower & Sweet Potato Bisque...........103

Enchilada Soup..104

Hearty Barley Stew..106

Pumpkin Lentil Stew...107

Spicy Carrot & Sweet Potato Soup.............................108

Spicy Chickpea & Tomato Stew..................................109

Split Second Split Pea Soup...111

Sweet Corn Chowder..112

Tipsy Onion Soup..114

White Bean & Tomato Bisque.....................................115

Wild Rice & Mushroom Soup.....................................117

Desserts..118

Almond Filled Peaches...118

Amaretto Cheesecake..119

Banana Nut Pudding..121

Black & Blue Berry Cobbler..122

Brown Rice & Pumpkin Pudding...............................124

Butterscotch Apple Bread Pudding...........................125

Caramel Filled Brownies..126

Caribbean Bread Pudding...128

Chocolate Peanut Butter Cheesecake......................129

Cookies 'N Cream Cake..131

Cranberry Apple Compote.. 132

French Cherry Pie...133

Glossy Orange Steamed Pudding...............................134

Green Tea Pudding..136

Lemonade Pie..138

Pina Colada Rice Pudding...139

Pineapple Carrot Cake... 140

Salted Caramel Apple Dip... 142

Mocha Café Steamed Pudding..................................... 143

Whiskey Pumpkin Cheesecake....................................144

White Chocolate Raspberry Bread Pudding........... 147

Introduction

Whether you have just decided to become a vegetarian or have been one for years, you may want some new ways to eat vegetables. This cookbook provides just that, with 100 recipes covering everything from appetizers and snacks to main dishes! Because we all want to indulge ourselves once in a while, I included a chapter on yummy desserts, too.

Before we get on to the good stuff, let's think about why choosing to give up meat is a good idea. (For those of you who have always been vegetarian, you may want to skip ahead, or keep reading and see if I have included anything you didn't already know).

Vegetarian vs. Vegan

These two words are often confused or used in the wrong way, so what exactly is the difference between them? Vegetarians have chosen to eat more healthily by eliminating meat from their diet while vegans have not only eliminated meat, but they won't consume anything with a face. Well, that sounds odd, doesn't it?

What I mean by that is, vegans don't eat any byproducts of animals. This means no eggs, dairy, or anything made with eggs or milk or butter. So, this cookbook is written for vegetarians, not vegans, although feel free to convert the recipes to fit your needs.

3 Types of Vegetarians: Which One Are You?

A no-meat diet is nothing new. People have chosen to not eat meat since at least 700 B.C., but over the past decade, more people are choosing to give up animal products in their diet. Some do it for health reasons and others, for ethical ones. No matter what your reason for choosing a vegetarian diet, you should know which type of vegetarian you are.

1. Folks who do not eat any animal flesh, which includes seafood, but do eat dairy and eggs are called lacto-ovo vegetarians.
2. Folks who do not eat meat or eggs, but do eat dairy, are called lacto vegetarians.
3. Folks who avoid meat and dairy but do eat eggs are called ovo vegetarians.

There is no right or wrong in these types; each is a personal choice which, in most cases, depends on why you chose to become a vegetarian in the first place. No matter which type you are, you will find many great health benefits that come with this type of diet.

Health Benefits of a Vegetarian Diet

Since a vegetarian diet is plant-based, it has a higher fiber content. It adds more folic acid, vitamins C and E, and plenty of essential nutrients, like magnesium. A plant-based diet is higher in unsaturated fat and contains many phytochemicals that help fight diseases like cancer. Most vegetarians do not have problems with obesity, have lower cholesterol and lower blood pressure. Let's take a look at four of the major benefits:

1. Better mood. Studies conducted at Benedictine University showed that restricting meat intake can improve your mood. One study showed a link between arachidonic acid, which is found in meat, and mood disturbances.
2. May improve psoriasis. A research study done at a Brazilian university found that eating a diet high in fruits and vegetables reduced the appearance of psoriasis.
3. May reduce onset of diabetes. According to George Washington University School of Medicine, a vegetarian diet helps manage diabetes and even reduce its onset by one half.
4. A study done at Nuffield Department of Clinical Medicine at the University of Oxford showed that vegetarians are less likely to develop cataracts later in life.

A vegetarian diet is rich in foods containing antioxidants, molecules that work to boost the immune system, which means being less likely to suffer from colds, flues, and other common illnesses.

Another benefit of a vegetarian diet, not related to your health, is saving money on groceries! Fruits, vegetables, and beans are much cheaper than beef, chicken or seafood.

Drawbacks to a Plant-Based Diet

While the benefits of a vegetarian diet are quite staggering, you should know there are some drawbacks, as well. With a little careful planning, a plant based diet can supply your body with all of the nutrients it needs, but eliminating meat also eliminates some protein and essential vitamins and minerals. You will need to make up for these by eating protein rich foods or taking a supplement.

Vitamins B12 and D, along with iron and calcium, are needed by the body and tend to be lacking in many vegetarian diets. You can find these in many plant foods by making sure that you eat plenty of protein-rich beans, quinoa, nuts, and tofu. Spinach and other leafy green vegetables are high in iron and calcium. Getting the right amounts of what your body needs is essential but not hard to do on a vegetarian diet. You will need to take a supplement for omega 3's as these are only found in fish and something you need to replace when you go green.

What You Can Expect in this Cookbook

By planning your daily meals using the recipes in the book, you can easily meet all of your nutritional needs. The recipes include a variety of ingredients from vegetables, fruits, nuts, seeds, tofu, and quinoa. For example, start your day with the Spiced Apple Quinoa, or Spinach & Quinoa Power Up. For lunch, enjoy a bowl of African Spicy Peanut Stew or Spicy Carrot & Sweet Potato Soup. Dinner could be something quick like Lightning Lo Mein or Split Second Split Pea Soup. When you want to go international, you can find recipes for that too, for example, Cauliflower Coconut Curry or Poblano & Zucchini Enchiladas will fit the bill. Need a good party appetizer or football Sunday snack? Try the Veggie Dumplings, Spicy Black Bean Dip or Ginger Tofu Pot Stickers.

When that sweet tooth needs satisfying, check out the chapter on desserts. You can find simple ones, like the Almond Filled Peaches, to the truly decadent like Chocolate Peanut Butter Cheesecake. There is even a recipe for Breakfast Bread Pudding or Peaches N Cream Coffee Cake to make weekend mornings special.

What is unique about the recipes in this book is that they are very easy and quick to make. The reason for this is that they were all designed to be made in the Instant Pot. If you don't know what that is, read on and you will quickly see that this is one small kitchen appliance you must have.

Instant Pot: What it is and Why You Need One

The Instant Pot may be the greatest kitchen appliances ever invented. This multi-use cooker speeds up cooking time, uses less energy, and replaces many of the kitchen devices you have now. The Instant Pot is a pressure cooker, rice steamer, and slow cooker; it sautés and can even be used to make yogurt.

The Instant Pot was developed by a team of Canadians in 2009. Their goal was to create an appliance that would help busy families eat a healthier diet. By developing a product that would cook nutritious meals in less time, more families would ditch fast food restaurants and go back to eating at home.

The first Instant Pot hit the market in 2010. The first one was designed with five kitchen tools compiled into one: pressure cooker, slow cooker, rice cooker, steamer, and warmer. The product was successful and continued to be improved. Over the succeeding years, new products came out in different sizes to serve smaller families and with added capability like the sauté function and yogurt maker.

Keeping up with advances in technology, in 2014, the first Instant Pot with Bluetooth technology was launched. This improvement allows you to program your cooker with your smartphone or other mobile device, with an app. Cooking just doesn't get any easier than this. In most cases, it takes more time to prepare the ingredients for your recipe than it does to cook it! Not only does this device make cooking faster and easier, cleaning up is a breeze. The main parts of the cooker are dishwasher safe, so no more scrubbing pots and pans!

Today, the company has many different cookers to choose from. Depending on your needs and the size of your family, you are likely to find one suited to you. Since these multi-use cookers are becoming so popular, it only follows that Instant Pot users will want new recipes and ways to use their Instant Pot. With that in mind, all the recipes in this cookbook use the Instant Pot in the cooking process.

You can use your Instant Pot to cook everything from breakfast to dinner, and believe it or not, you can even use it to create stunning, delicious desserts like cheesecakes, steamed puddings, and pies. You will find recipes for all of these in the chapters that follow.

Appetizers & Snacks
Easy Cheesy Beer Dip

One of the trendy new dips served by many of the big restaurants is the cheesy beer dip. Now, you can make this tasty treat at home. Serve with pretzel rods, crackers or vegetables.

Serves: 4

Time: 20 minutes

Ingredients:
- 4 cups grated sharp cheddar cheese
- 1 cup beer or ale
- 2 tablespoons cornstarch
- 2 tablespoons butter
- 2 cloves garlic, finely chopped

Method:
1. Set Instant Pot to sauté. Add butter and let melt.
2. Once butter is melted, add garlic and cook 1-2 minutes. Stir in cornstarch and whisk till the mixture forms a roux.
3. Add half the cheese and beer, stirring till combined.
4. Add remaining cheese, slowly, stirring constantly till cheese has melted and dip is smooth.
5. Serve immediately or keep warm in a mini crockpot.

Eggplant Bruschetta

This versatile appetizer will be the hit at any party! Make according to directions for a tasty treat or process in a blender or food processor and serve as a dip with chips or crackers.

Serves: 4-6

Time: 2 hours 15 minutes

Ingredients:

- 3 cups eggplant, chopped
- 1 ½ cups tomatoes, diced
- 1 6 oz. can of green olives, pits removed and chopped
- 1 loaf of French or Italian bread
- 1 tablespoon fresh basil, chopped fine
- 2 teaspoon capers
- 4 cloves garlic, chopped fine
- 2 teaspoons balsamic vinegar
- Salt & pepper to taste

Method:

1. Place all of the ingredients except the bread and vinegar in the inner pot.
2. Set the Instant Pot to slow cooker and the timer for 2 hours.

3. Before the vegetables are finished cooking, slice the bread into ½ inch slices. Toast the bread, on both sides, under the broiler.
4. When the vegetables are done stir in the vinegar. Top the toasted bread slices with one tablespoon of the eggplant mixture. Serve.

Fried Garlic Potato Ravioli

Most folks think that ravioli is difficult to make. But, that is not the case with these scrumptious darlings. Your guests will be totally impressed when they learn you made these yourself. Serve with marinara sauce or dip of your choice.

Serves: 4-6
Time: 90 minutes
Ingredients:
For the Dough:
- 1 ½ cups flour
- 2 large eggs
- ½ teaspoon salt

For the Filling:
- 4-5 red potatoes, peeled, cooked, and mashed
- ½ cup feta cheese, crumbled
- 3 cloves garlic, chopped fine

- 1 teaspoon fresh dill, chopped fine
- ¾ teaspoon salt

Method:
1. For the dough: mix flour and salt in large mixing bowl. Add the eggs, one at a time, mixing with a fork. When dough starts to form, use your hands to continue kneading. The dough should be smooth but not sticky. Wrap in plastic and chill one hour.
2. For the filling: in a large bowl, mix all of the ingredients until combined. Set aside.
3. When dough has chilled, roll out to 1/8-inch thickness on lightly floured board. Cut into 3-inch squares.
4. Take 1 tablespoon of filling mixture and shape into a ball. Flatten slightly and place on a dough square. Top with another square of dough and seal the edges firmly. Repeat, using all of the dough and filling.
5. Cook the ravioli in small batches to keep them from sticking together. Place 2 cups of water in the inner pot of your cooker and add about 1/3 of the raviolis. Add lid and lock in place. Set to manual and cook for 3 minutes. Use the quick release and remove ravioli with a slotted spoon; set aside. Repeat until all raviolis are cooked.
6. Empty the water from the inner pot and wipe dry. Set to sauté function and add 1-2 tablespoons of butter.

When butter is hot and melted, fry raviolis on both sides till nicely browned and crispy.

Ginger Tofu Pot Stickers

Pot stickers are an Asian dumpling traditionally made from pork, but now, you can enjoy these popular appetizers at home. These savory dumplings are filled with seasoned tofu, ginger, and garlic and will melt in your mouth.

Yields: 18
Time: 30 mins
Ingredients:
- ½ lb. extra firm tofu
- 1 scallion, chopped
- 1 tablespoon soy sauce
- ½ tablespoon olive oil
- 1 clove garlic, chopped fine
- ½ teaspoon fresh ginger, grated
- 15-20 wonton wrappers

Method:
1. Prepare tofu: wrap tofu in paper towels and place on a plate. Use something heavy to "press" the tofu to release the excess water.
2. Set your cooker to sauté. Add oil and heat until hot. Add ginger and garlic and cook 1 minute.

3. Crumble the tofu into the garlic mixture and cook, stirring occasionally, 5 minutes. Stir in scallion; remove the mixture from the pot and set aside.
4. Place one wrapper with point towards you. Add 1 teaspoon of filling to center. Moisten the edges of the wrapper and fold bottom corner upwards, then side corners inward to meet the bottom corner. Fold top corner down and seal edges firmly. Repeat with remaining wrappers and filling.
5. Place in bamboo steamer, if you have one, or use the steamer basket. Place in cooker and set to steam. Add lid and lock in place. Steam for 5 minutes or until outside looks shiny. Use quick release to remove the lid. Serve with soy sauce.

Greek Feta Dip

This creamy, cheesy dip has all the flavors of the Mediterranean. Yogurt with feta cheese and fresh mint, not the traditional dip found on most appetizer tables. Serve with fresh vegetables or crackers.

Serves: 8-10
Time: 20 minutes
Ingredients:
- 1 cup Greek yogurt, not flavored
- 2/3 cup feta cheese, crumbled

- ½ cup cream cheese, cut into cubes
- 4 tablespoons olive oil
- 2 tablespoon fresh mint, chopped
- 2 cloves garlic, peeled and crushed
- 1 teaspoon lemon zest

Method:
1. Spray the inner pot with cooking spray.
2. Place the yogurt, cheeses, oil, and garlic into pot. Mix thoroughly.
3. Add lid and using the Slow Cooker function, cook on low 20 minutes or until cheese has melted.
4. Remove dip from pot and stir in the mint and lemon zest. Serve.

Kale & Ginger Spring Rolls

These healthy spring rolls will be the hit at any party: ideal for summer potlucks or served at backyard BBQ's and so yummy even the kids will eat them. Serve them with or without dipping sauce.

Serves: 6

Time: 60 minutes

Ingredients:
- 6-8 shiitake mushrooms, chopped
- 1 small yellow onion, chopped fine
- 1 ½ cups carrot, grated

- 1 cup Napa cabbage, sliced thin
- 1 cup kale, sliced thin
- ¼ cup soy sauce
- 1 scallion, chopped fine
- 1 clove garlic, chopped fine
- 4 tablespoons coconut oil
- 1 tablespoon rice vinegar
- 1 teaspoon fresh ginger, grated
- 1 teaspoon sesame oil
- 12 spring roll wrappers

Method:
1. Set cooker to sauté and heat 1 tablespoon of the oil till hot.
2. Add onions and cook 2 minutes. Add in garlic, ginger, mushrooms and carrot and cook 3 minutes more, stirring frequently.
3. Add the kale, cabbage, and scallions and continue cooking 3 more minutes.
4. Mix together soy sauce, sesame oil, and vinegar in a small bowl. Pour into the skillet and mix to coat the vegetables. Remove from pot and let cool slightly.
5. Place wrapper on work surface so one corner points towards you. Place 2 tablespoons of filling mixture in center, forming a line. Fold the sides inwards and

bottom corner up. Moisten the top corner and roll up burrito style.
6. Clean the pot and add the remaining oil. Heat until hot.
7. Cook the spring rolls in small batches, 2-5 minutes per side. Roll and continue cooking until golden brown. Remove from pot and drain on paper towels.
8. Serve with or without dipping sauce.

Mini Black Bean Burgers

Even though you've decided to go green, that doesn't mean you can't enjoy a great burger. These easy-to-make patties are so delicious even the carnivores will love them. Make into mini burgers for appetizers or full size for dinner!

Serves: 6 mini burgers
Time: 1 hour 15 minutes
Ingredients:
- 1 15 oz. can black beans, rinsed and drained well
- 6 mini burger rolls
- ½ cup tortilla chips, crushed
- ½ large avocado, cut into 6 slices
- ½ cup mayo
- ½ cup salsa
- 1 large egg
- 1 chipotle in adobo, chopped fine

- 2 tablespoons dried minced onion
- 2 tablespoons flour
- 2 tablespoons olive oil
- 1 teaspoon sea salt
- 1 ¼ teaspoons cumin, divided
- ½ teaspoon red chili flakes
- ½ teaspoon garlic powder
- ½ teaspoon paprika

Method:
1. Place the beans, tortilla chips, egg, onion, flour, salt, 1 teaspoon cumin, chili flakes, garlic powder, and paprika in a food processor. Process until ingredients are pureed, but be sure to keep some texture. Transfer to a bowl and cover with plastic wrap. Chill for one hour.
2. In a small bowl, combine mayo, chipotle and remaining ¼ teaspoon of cumin, set aside.
3. Set your cooker to sauté and heat the olive oil.
4. Divide the bean mixture into 6 portions and shape into patties about 2 inches around and ½ inch thick. Place in cooker and fry 3-5 minutes on each side. Remove from cooker and drain on paper towels.
5. Split the burger rolls and spread the top half with mayo mixture, add bean patty, top with salsa and slice of avocado. Serve.

Roasted Garlic Hummus

Using roasted garlic cloves in a traditional hummus recipe adds new depths of flavor. Serve with vegetables, pita chips, or as a great sauce for pasta!

Yields: 1 quart of hummus

Time: 1 hour 15 minutes

Ingredients:
- 1 ½ cups dried chickpeas (not soaked)
- 2 ½ - 3 cups water
- ½ cup tahini
- 1 head of garlic
- 3 tablespoons fresh lemon juice
- 1 - 1 ½ teaspoon olive oil
- 1 ½ teaspoon sea salt
- ½ teaspoon baking soda
- ¼ teaspoon black pepper

Method:
1. Add chickpeas, water, and baking soda to the Instant Pot. Set to manual and the time to 55 minutes.
2. Heat oven to 425 degrees. Cut the top off the garlic and the top off each clove. Place on foil, drizzle well with olive oil, and sprinkle with ½ tsp. salt. Wrap tightly and bake for 30 minutes or until the garlic is golden on top. Let cool while chickpeas finish cooking.

3. When the timer is done, let the pressure release naturally.
4. Strain the chickpeas, reserving the cooking liquid.
5. Add chickpeas, 2-3 cloves of the roasted garlic, tahini, lemon juice, 1 tsp. salt and pepper to a food processor. Process until combined, adding reserved cooking liquid, if needed, to achieve desired consistency.
6. Scrape into serving bowl and garnish as desired.

Spicy Black Bean Dip

This foolproof bean dip makes a great appetizer for those holiday parties. Easy to prepare, yet your guests will think you spent hours cooking it. Serve warm with tortilla chips or crackers for dipping.

Serves: 8
Time: 60 minutes
Ingredients:
- 4 cups water
- 2 cups dried black beans, rinsed and drained well
- 2 cups vegetable broth
- 1 medium sweet onion, chopped fine
- ½ cup cream cheese, cut into cubes
- ½ cup sharp cheddar cheese, grated
- 2 cloves garlic, peeled and chopped fine
- 2 tablespoons fresh cilantro, chopped

- 1 tablespoon smoked paprika
- 1 tablespoon ground cumin
- ½ teaspoon salt

Method:
1. Add all ingredients except the cheeses to the Instant Pot. Add the lid and lock. Press Manual and adjust time to 25 minutes pressure cooking. When done, open the Instant Pot using natural pressure release.
2. Heat oven to 400 degrees. Mash the beans with a potato masher to desired consistency. Stir in the cream cheese and half of the cheddar cheese.
3. Transfer mixture to an 8x8 baking dish and top with remaining cheddar cheese.
4. Bake about 20 minutes or until cheese is melted and starting to brown.
5. Garnish as desired and serve warm.

Spicy Tofu Lettuce Wraps

Yummy little appetizers that look almost as good as they taste! Make some up for watching sports on the weekends or double the recipe if you are serving them at a party. They also make a great lunch item.

Serves: 3 to 4
Time: 45 minutes
Ingredients:

- 2 ½ cups water
- 2 cups brown rice, uncooked
- 1 package firm tofu
- 2 carrots, peeled and grated
- 1 cup frozen corn
- ½ cup cashew halves
- 3 tablespoons soy sauce
- 1 tablespoon chili powder
- 1 tablespoon olive oil
- ½ teaspoon Sriracha
- Several small heads of young lettuce; wash and separate leaves

Method:
1. Place water and rice into the inner pot of your cooker. Close and lock lid. Press Manual and set timer to 22 minutes. When timer goes off, use the natural pressure release to remove the lid.
2. Meanwhile, press tofu for 15 minutes to remove excess water.
3. Remove rice from pot and wipe clean. Set the cooker to sauté and add the olive oil to heat.
4. Crumble the tofu into the oil, breaking it down into very small pieces. Cook for about 15 minutes, stirring frequently, until nicely brown.

5. Add corn and cook, stirring, until most of the liquid has evaporated, about 3-4 minutes. Add chili powder and cashews and stir to mix.
6. Add soy sauce and Sriracha, and cook, stirring constantly till liquid is absorbed. Remove from heat.
7. To serve, place scoop of rice and scoop of tofu mixture on lettuce leaf. Add some carrot and roll up.

Spinach & Asiago Dip

One of the most popular dips today, this creamy dip is very simple to make. Serve warm with chips, vegetables or crackers.

Serves: 10
Time: 70 minutes
Ingredients:
- 4 cups asiago cheese, grated
- 2 8-oz. blocks of cream cheese, cut into cubes
- ¾ cup baby spinach, coarsely chopped
- 1 teaspoon garlic powder
- ½ teaspoon Italian seasoning

Method:
1. Spray inner pot with cooking spray. Add all ingredients to the pot. Close and lock lid.

2. Set to slow cooker function and timer to 60 minutes. When timer goes off, use natural release to remove lid. Stir well and serve warm.

Sweet Potato Quesadillas

Aww, quesadillas, one of the most perfect finger foods. Not only are these quesadillas easy to prepare, they pack a ton of health benefits in every bite!

Serves: 6-8

Time: 35 minutes

Ingredients:
- 4 cups sweet potato, peeled and grated
- 1½ cups onion, chopped fine
- 1 cup Monterey Jack cheese, grated
- 2 garlic cloves, chopped fine
- 1 lime, halved
- 5 tablespoons olive oil, divided
- 1 ½ teaspoons cumin
- 1 teaspoon chili powder
- 1/8 teaspoon cayenne
- Salt and pepper to taste
- 8 small tortillas

Method:

1. Set cooker to sauté and add 3 tablespoons of oil. Add onions and cook until translucent, about 3-5 minutes.
2. Add sweet potatoes and spices and cook, covered, about 10 minutes, stirring frequently. When the potatoes are tender, squeeze half a lime over them and salt and pepper to taste. Remove from pot and wipe clean.
3. Heat remaining oil. Fill tortillas with potato mixture and add cheese. Fold in half and cook, 2-3 minutes per side, until nicely browned. Repeat.
4. Serve with sour cream for dipping, if you like.

Sweet & Spicy Cheesy Corn Dip

A different take on the classic bean and cheese dip. The sweet corn helps to mellow out the heat of the jalapeno so this dip can be enjoyed by most. Serve with tortilla chips or crackers.

Serves: 4

Time: 40 minutes

Ingredients:

- 2 cups sweet corn, frozen
- 1 cup cream cheese with chives & onions, cut into cubes
- ½ cup Monterrey Jack cheese, grated
- ½ cup Parmesan cheese, grated

- 1 jalapeno, seeded and chopped
- ½ teaspoon garlic powder

Method:
1. Spray the inner pot with cooking spray. Add in all ingredients.
2. Add lid and lock in place. Use the slow cooker function and set timer to 30 minutes or cook until the cheese has melted.
3. Transfer to serving dish and serve warm.

Veggie Dumplings

Delicate dumplings that are packed full of healthy ingredients. Best if steamed in a bamboo basked, or line the steamer basket of your cooker with parchment paper. Serve with the sweet chili sauce for dipping.

Yields: 20

Time: 40-60 minutes

Ingredients:
- 1 ½ cups of cabbage, sliced thin
- 1 cup mushrooms, chopped fine
- 1 small carrot, peeled and chopped fine
- 2 green onions, chopped fine
- 1 tablespoon of soy sauce
- 2 cloves garlic, chopped fine
- 1 teaspoon of sesame oil

- 1 teaspoon of sweet chili sauce
- 20 fresh wonton wrappers

Method:
1. Set the cooker to sauté and heat the oil. Add garlic and vegetables and cook about 5 minutes, stirring frequently. Remove from pot and place in large bowl.
2. Add soy sauce and chili sauce and stir to coat the vegetables. Let cool completely.
3. Place wrapper on work surface and spoon 2 teaspoons of filling onto center. Lift up sides of wrapper and twist to enclose the filling. Repeat.
4. Arrange dumplings in single layer of steamer basket (you will need to steam these in batches). Place in cooker, close and lock lid and set to steam, setting timer for 10 minutes. When timer goes off, remove lid with quick release. Repeat. Serve with dipping sauce.

Breakfast Recipes

Banana Chocolate Rice Pudding

This rice pudding will get the kids out of bed, and it's quick enough to make that you will have plenty of time to get ready for your day, too. Just let your Instant Pot do all the work! Serve with banana slices and/or walnuts.

Serves: 4-6

Time: 15 minutes

Ingredients:

- 4 cups of chocolate banana milk
- 1 cup of arborio rice
- 2 eggs
- 1 teaspoon pure vanilla extract
- ½ teaspoon salt

Method:

1. Place milk, rice, vanilla, and salt into the inner pot of your cooker. Whisk in the eggs. Set to low pressure and close and lock lid. Set the timer for 12 minutes. When the timer goes off remove the lid with natural release. Serve with or without desired toppings.

Breakfast Bread Pudding

Pudding for breakfast? Why not? This breakfast pudding has less sugar than a stack of pancakes or French toast. And the warm flavors of cinnamon and orange marmalade will keep you going all day.

Serves: 4-6

Time: 25 minutes

Ingredients:

- 5 cups bread cubes
- 1 cup milk
- 2 large eggs, beaten well

- ¼ cup orange marmalade
- ¼ cup sugar
- ¼ cup raisins
- 2 teaspoons vanilla
- ½ teaspoon ground cinnamon

Method:
1. Lightly butter a tall baking dish, which will fit inside your Instant Pot. Set aside.
2. Place rack in bottom of inner pot with 2 cups of water.
3. In a large bowl, combine all ingredients except the bread and raisins. Mix until smooth. Add bread and raisins and stir well so bread soaks up the liquids.
4. Pour mixture into prepared baking dish. Cover with foil. Using a foil sling, place dish on rack in cooker. Fold down the ends of sling.
5. Close and lock the lid. Set to high pressure; once high pressure is reached, reduce to low. Set timer for 15 minutes.
6. When timer goes off, remove lid with quick release. Unfold ends of foil sling and remove baking dish from cooker. Remove foil and let pudding cool for 5 minutes.
7. Garnish with your favorite fresh berries and serve.

Cheesy Tater Tot Casserole

Simple to prepare and oh so delicious to eat. Start this cheesy breakfast casserole early while everyone is still sleeping. You can also prepare it and reheat it later as needed.

Serves: 4

Time: 90 minutes

Ingredients:
- 1 large bag of Tater Tots, frozen
- 6 large eggs
- 1 cup medium cheddar cheese, grated
- 2 tablespoon heavy cream
- ½ teaspoon garlic powder
- ½ teaspoon dried thyme
- ¼ teaspoon salt
- ⅛ teaspoon pepper

Method:
1. Spray the inner pot of the Instant Pot with cooking spray.
2. Place about two thirds of the tater tots in the pot.
3. In a medium bowl, whisk together eggs, cream, and spices and pour over the tots.
4. Add remaining tater tots and top with grated cheese.

5. Close and lock the lid. Turn steam release to Venting. Select the Slow Cook function and set to 60 minutes cooking time.
6. Serve with salt and pepper to taste.

Fall French Toast Casserole

This easy to make casserole will be perfect for the holidays: a take on French toast with a favorite fall fruit, pumpkin! Perfect for those crisp, cold fall mornings.

Serves: 6-8
Time: 2 hours, 10 minutes
Ingredients:
- 1 loaf French bread, cut into cubes
- 2 cups canned pumpkin
- 2 cups half and half
- 5 eggs
- 1 teaspoon ground cinnamon
- ½ teaspoon ground nutmeg
- 1/8 teaspoon salt
- 1/8 teaspoon cloves, ground

Topping:
- ¼ cup butter
- ¼ cup brown sugar

- ½ teaspoon ground cinnamon
- ¼ teaspoon ground nutmeg
- 1/8 teaspoon cloves, ground

Method:
1. Spray the inner pot of the Instant Pot with cooking spray.
2. Place the bread cubes in the pot.
3. In medium bowl, whisk together pumpkin, half and half, eggs, and spices until thoroughly combined. Pour over bread cubes.
4. Place the topping ingredients in a small bowl. Mix with fork until combined and crumbly. Sprinkle over mixture in the pot.
5. Cover inner pot with foil, being sure to smooth it down the side of the pot.
6. Using a small, sharp knife, cut 1 1/4-inch-long slits in the foil, about one inch from the edge, at the four points of the clock, 3, 6, 9 and 12.
7. Place pot in the cooker and close and lock lid. Set steam release to vent. Cook on slow-cooker function for about 90 minutes.
8. Release pressure and serve while hot. Drizzle with syrup if desired.

Mediterranean Baked Eggs

What this breakfast lacks in beauty, it makes up for in taste. Healthy, quick to prepare meal that is great for weekend brunches.

Serves: 6-8

Time: 1 hour 10 minutes

Ingredients:

- 12 large eggs, well beaten
- 3 cups sourdough bread, cut into cubes
- 1 cup fresh spinach, rinsed, drained, and chopped
- ¾ cup milk
- ½ cup sun-dried tomatoes; pat dry with paper towel and chop
- ½ cup feta cheese, crumbled
- ½ teaspoon garlic powder
- ½ teaspoon salt
- ¼ teaspoon onion powder
- ¼ teaspoon black pepper

Method:

1. Spray the inner pot of the Instant Pot with cooking spray.
2. Place bread cubes in the pot. Top with spinach, cheese and tomatoes.

3. In large mixing bowl, beat eggs, milk, and seasonings until thoroughly combined.
4. Pour egg mixture over ingredients in the pot, making sure all the bread is covered.
5. Close and lock the lid. Turn steam release to Venting. Select the Slow Cook function and set to 60 minutes cooking time.
6. Release lid and serve.

Not So Scotch Eggs

Scotch eggs are usually hard-boiled, wrapped in sausage, dipped in bread crumbs and fried to golden perfection. Here is a recipe that mimics those fabulous flavors, without the sausage, of course. Serve for weekend brunch, or they make great appetizers, too.

Serves: 4

Time: 40 minutes

Ingredients:
- 4 large eggs, boiled and peeled
- 4 cups canned chickpeas, rinsed and drained well
- 1½ cups panko breadcrumbs
- 2 green onions, sliced
- ½ cup vegetable oil
- ⅓ cup flour
- 1 large egg, raw

- 1 tablespoon Dijon mustard
- 1 tablespoon dried oregano
- ¾ tsp salt

Method:
1. Set cooker to sauté and add oil to heat.
2. Place chickpeas, onions, mustard, and seasonings in a food processor. Process until the mixture becomes a chunky paste, about 20-30 seconds.
3. Scoop out a fourth of the chickpea paste and flatten with your hand. Place one boiled egg in the center and wrap the paste around it. Repeat.
4. In a small bowl, whisk the egg well.
5. Place the flour on one plate, and the bread crumbs on another.
6. Dip each egg in the flour, then raw egg and, lastly, the breadcrumbs. Repeat with all the eggs.
7. Cook the eggs in the hot oil, 2-3 minutes, turning occasionally, until nicely brown. Remove from oil and drain on paper towels. Serve.

Peaches 'N Cream Coffee Cake

Make mornings extraordinary when you serve this whole grain, protein-rich breakfast cake. The kids will be so happy to have cake for breakfast that they don't need to know it's good for them!

Serves: 6

Time: 60 mins

Ingredients:

For the cake:

- 1 cup white whole wheat flour
- 5 eggs
- ¾ cup plain or vanilla yogurt
- ¾ cup ricotta cheese
- ½ cup Peach Compote, chilled (recipe follows)
- ¼ cup sugar
- 2 tablespoons butter, melted
- 2 teaspoons baking powder
- 2 teaspoons vanilla
- ½ teaspoon salt

For the glaze:

- ¼ cup yogurt
- 1-2 tablespoons powdered sugar
- 1 teaspoon milk
- ½ teaspoon vanilla

Method:
1. For the cake, spray a 6-cup Bundt pan with cooking spray.
2. In a large bowl, beat together the eggs and sugar until smooth. Add butter, ricotta, yogurt and vanilla and continue beating until batter is smooth.
3. In a separate bowl, stir together dry ingredients. Add to batter and stir until thoroughly combined. Pour into prepared pan.
4. Drop the peach compote, by tablespoons, on top of the batter and marble with a knife.
5. Place a trivet or rack on the bottom of the inner pot of your cooker. Add 1 cup of water. Place the cake on the trivet.
6. Close and lock the lid. Cook on high pressure and set timer for 25 minutes. When timer goes off, use natural release to remove the lid.
7. For the glaze, whisk all ingredients together until smooth.
8. Remove cake from the cooker and let cool slightly. Loosen sides and turn, gently, onto serving plate. Drizzle with glaze and serve.

Peach Compote

Once you taste this compote you will want to keep it on hand. Use it to top desserts, swirl into yogurt, or mix in your morning oatmeal. Heck, you will probably want to eat it with just a spoon!

Yields: 2 cups
Time: 20 minutes
Ingredients:

- 4 cups peaches, peeled and chopped
- 2 tablespoons water, divided
- ½ tablespoon cornstarch
- 1 teaspoon vanilla

Method:

1. Place peaches, 1 tablespoon water, and vanilla into inner pot of cooker. Close and lock lid. Set on high pressure and set timer for 1 minute.
2. When timer goes off, remove lid with natural release for 5 minutes, then release remaining pressure.
3. Set the cooker to sauté and bring peaches to a simmer. Mix cornstarch with remaining tablespoon of water and add to peaches. Cook, stirring constantly, for 1 minute or until thickened.
4. Let cool and store in airtight container in the refrigerator for up to one week.

South of the Border Baked Eggs

Spicy, tasty dish that will leave your guests begging for more. This egg casserole is perfect for a potluck or weekend brunch. If your family doesn't like spicy foods, leave out the jalapeno.

Serves: 4-6

Time: 20 minutes

Ingredients:

- 1 15 oz.-can black beans, drained and rinsed well
- 1 14.5 oz. can tomatoes, finely chopped
- 1 4 oz. can green chilies, finely diced
- 4 - 6 eggs
- 1 small onion, finely chopped
- ½ a jalapeno, seeds removed, finely diced
- ¼ cup cheddar cheese, grated
- 1 tablespoon olive oil
- ½ teaspoon ground cumin
- ¼ teaspoon chili pepper
- fresh cilantro, finely chopped for garnish

Method:

1. Set your Instant Pot to Sauté and keep the temperature at normal. Add olive oil and heat until hot. Add onion and jalapeno and cook, stirring frequently, about 2

minutes. Add cumin and chili pepper and cook another minute more.
2. Add tomatoes, beans, and green chilies, place the lid on the pot, and cook on high pressure 8-10 minutes until the mixture has thickened.
3. Use the back of a cooking spoon to make 4-6 wells in the bean mixture. Crack an egg in each of the wells. Top with grated cheese.
4. Place the lid back on the pot and cook on high pressure 4-5 minutes, until eggs are set and cheese is melted.
5. Release lid and serve garnished with chopped cilantro. You can also garnish with a dollop of sour cream and serve with warm tortillas.

Spiced Apple Quinoa

Warm and comforting, a great way to start a cold, winter's day. Not only is it quick to make, but it's packed with great health benefits for the body.

Serves: 4
Time: 10 minutes
Ingredients:
- 2 ½ cups milk
- 1 cup red quinoa, uncooked
- 2 large apples, peeled, cored, and chopped
- 2 teaspoons cinnamon

- maple syrup

Method:
1. Place all ingredients, except syrup, in the pressure cooker. Close and lock lid. Set to manual and set timer for 2 minutes.
2. When timer goes off, use the quick release to remove lid. Ladle into bowls and drizzle with syrup. Serve immediately.

Spinach & Quinoa Power Up

This simple breakfast packs a healthy punch. Warm, filling, and easy to prepare. Perfect for those busy mornings when you have no time to cook.

Serves: 4
Time: 90 minutes
Ingredients:
- 1½ cups milk
- 6 large eggs
- ½ cup raw quinoa, rinsed well
- ¾ cup roasted red peppers, chopped
- ½ cup fresh spinach, chopped
- ¼ cup Parmesan cheese, grated
- ¼ cup Monterey Jack cheese, grated
- ½ teaspoon sea salt

- 1/8 teaspoon black pepper

Method:
1. Spray the inner pot of the Instant Pot with cooking spray.
2. In a medium bowl, beat eggs. Add quinoa, milk, and seasonings and mix until combined.
3. Fold in vegetables and Monterey Jack cheese.
4. Pour into inner pot and top with Parmesan cheese.
5. Close and lock the lid. Turn steam release to Venting. Select the Slow Cook function and set to 60 minutes cooking time.
6. Release lid and serve.

Steel Cut Carrot Cake

This rich oatmeal is packed with all of the flavors of Grandma's carrot cake. You'll feel like you are eating cake for breakfast but know that it's good for you. Tastes so good even the kids will love it!

Serves: 6
Time: 40 mins
Ingredients:
- 4 cups water
- 1 cup steel cut oats
- 1 cup carrots, grated
- ¾ cup raisins

- ¼ cup chia seeds
- 3 tablespoons maple syrup
- 1 tablespoon butter
- 2 teaspoons cinnamon
- 1 teaspoon pumpkin pie spice
- ¼ teaspoon salt

Method:
1. Set cooker to sauté and add butter. Once butter has melted, add oats and sauté, stirring constantly, about 3 minutes.
2. Add water, carrots, syrup, and spices. Set to high pressure, and set timer for 10 minutes.
3. When timer goes off, remove lid with natural release for 10 minutes, then finish with quick release.
4. Stir in raisins and chia. Cover and let rest for 5 minutes or until oatmeal is desired thickness. Garnish with additional raisins and serve immediately.

Super Scrambled Breakfast Tacos

Most of us are familiar with breakfast burritos, so, why not breakfast tacos?! Packed full of protein, vitamins, and essential nutrients to keep you going all day.

Serves: 4
Time: 30 minutes
Ingredients:

- 7 large eggs, well beaten
- 1 medium sweet potato, peeled and chopped
- 1/3 cup spinach
- ½ cup black beans, rinsed and drained well
- 1 ripe avocado, peeled and sliced
- 3 tablespoons olive oil
- 1 teaspoon chili powder
- Salt and pepper to taste
- 6-8 corn tortillas

Method:
1. Set the cooker to sauté and add the oil. Once the oil is hot, add sweet potato. Cover and cook, stirring frequently, about 15 minutes.
2. While the potatoes are cooking, warm the tortillas in a 350-degree oven, wrapped in foil. Heat beans in a small pot and keep warm.
3. When the potatoes are tender, add the spinach and cook another 2 minutes. Stir in seasonings.
4. Pour beaten eggs over potato mixture and cook, stirring frequently to scramble. Cook until eggs reach desired consistency.
5. To assemble the tacos: remove tortillas from foil and add beans. Top with potato mixture and slice of avocado. Serve with your favorite salsa.

Tofu & Pepper Breakfast Burrito

Another south-of-the-border breakfast treat! These breakfast burritos are a great option for taking breakfast with you. Just wrap some foil around the bottom and you are ready to go.

Serves: 5

Time: 40 minutes

Ingredients:

- 1 package extra firm tofu, pressed for 15 minutes and cut into cubes
- 2 red bell peppers, seeds and ribs removed, then sliced
- 1 onion, sliced
- ½ cup kidney beans, rinsed and drained
- 1 avocado, sliced
- ¼ cup vegetable broth
- ¼ cup salsa
- 1 tablespoon oil
- 1 teaspoon turmeric
- ½ teaspoon cumin
- salt and pepper
- 5 flour tortillas

Method:

1. Set cooker to sauté and add oil. Once oil is hot, add peppers and onion and cook about 15 minutes, stirring occasionally. Remove and set aside.

2. Add the tofu, spices and broth. Cook, stirring occasionally, about 7 minutes, or until the broth is absorbed. Add beans; cook and stir 2-4 minutes.
3. To make burritos, spoon tofu mixture onto tortilla, add pepper mix, and top with slice of avocado and salsa. Roll up and enjoy.

Zucchini Breakfast Quiche

The secret to this quiche is to prep the zucchini the same way as tofu. Slice it thinly and sprinkle with salt. Let sit 20-30 minutes, then place in cheesecloth and squeeze out excess water. This will prevent your quiche from being soggy.

Serves: 6-8
Time: 90 minutes
Ingredients:
- 2 lbs. zucchini, excess water removed
- 2 cups cheddar cheese, grated
- 1 ½ cup milk
- 2 eggs
- salt and pepper

Method:
1. Whisk eggs and milk together in a mixing bowl. Add salt and pepper to taste. Stir in 1 cup of the cheese.

2. Spray the inner pot of the cooker with cooking spray. Place half the zucchini slices in an even layer on the bottom. Sprinkle ½ cup cheese over the top.
3. Add the remaining zucchini, in an even layer, and pour egg mixture over top. Finish with remaining cheese.
4. Close and lock lid. Select slow cooker function and set time for 60 minutes. When timer goes off, remove lid with quick release. Serve.

Main Dishes

Asian Style Sautéed Eggplant

Eggplant, when cooked properly, has an almost meaty texture. It is a good substitute for tofu. This recipe offers the texture of a meat patty with yummy Asian flavors. Serve with brown rice and a salad.

Serves: 4
Time: 90 minutes
Ingredients:

- 1 large eggplant, sliced in fourths
- 3 green onions, chopped, green tips only
- ¼ cup + 1 teaspoon cornstarch
- 1 tablespoon vegetable oil
- 1 ½ tablespoons soy sauce
- 1 ½ tablespoons sesame oil

- 1 tablespoon fish sauce
- 2 teaspoons sugar
- 1 teaspoon fresh ginger, chopped fine
- ¼ teaspoon salt
- 1/16 teaspoon wheat-free asafetida powder

Method:
1. Lay sliced eggplant on paper towels. Sprinkle both sides with salt and let set for 1 hour. Then pat dry with more paper towels.
2. In a small mixing bowl, whisk together soy sauce, sesame oil, fish sauce, sugar, 1 teaspoon cornstarch, and the asafetida powder.
3. Use the ¼ cup of cornstarch to coat both sides of sliced eggplant; use more cornstarch if needed.
4. Set cooker to sauté and add vegetable oil. Once hot, add ½ the ginger and 1 green onion, lay 2 slices of eggplant over top. Use ½ the sauce mixture to lightly coat both sides of the eggplant, cook 8-10 minutes per side. Repeat with remaining ingredients.
5. Garnish with remaining sliced green onions and serve.

Cannellini in Tomato Sauce

Protein packed meal with the flavors of the Mediterranean. You can substitute the cannellini with any other white bean, just remember to adjust the cooking time. Garnish with crumbled feta cheese, red pepper flakes, and a squeeze of fresh lemon juice. Serve with a salad and crusty bread to soak up all the sauce.

Serves: 6
Time: 90 minutes
Ingredients:
- 5 cups water
- 2½ cups dried cannellini beans
- 2 ½ cups canned whole peeled tomatoes, drained
- 1 medium onion, chopped
- 4 cloves garlic, sliced thin
- ½ cup dry white wine
- ¼ cup olive oil, plus more
- 1 tablespoon sea salt, plus more
- 2 bay leaves
- ½ teaspoon crushed red pepper flakes

Method:
1. Set cooker to sauté and add oil. Once oil gets hot add onion and cook, stirring frequently, 5-8 minutes, or until onion is translucent. Add garlic and red pepper flakes and sauté another 2 minutes.
2. Add wine and bring to boil. Cook about 5 minutes, or until wine has evaporated.

3. Add beans, bay leaves, salt, and water. Close and lock the lid. Select the manual setting and set timer for 50 minutes.
4. When timer goes off, use quick release to remove lid. If beans are not tender, replace lid and cook another 10 minutes.
5. Add tomatoes, breaking up with spoon, and sauté, stirring frequently, until sauce has thickened, about 25-30 minutes. Season with more salt if needed. Serve.

Cauliflower Coconut Curry

Curry is a spice found in almost all Indian dishes. It adds a warm heat and tons of flavor. If spicy is not your thing, reduce the amount of curry in this recipe. Serve over steamed rice.

Serves: 6
Time: 35 minutes
Ingredients:
- 1 medium head cauliflower, separated into small florets
- 2 10 oz. cans diced tomatoes with green chilies
- 15 oz. can garbanzo beans, rinsed and drained well
- 1 ¾ cups unsweet coconut milk
- 2 onions, cut into 1/2-inch pieces
- ½ cup fresh cilantro, chopped

- 2 tablespoons vegetable oil
- 5 teaspoons curry powder
- Salt and pepper to taste

Method:
1. Set cooker to sauté and add oil. Once the oil is hot, add onions and cook 8 minutes or till golden brown.
2. Add curry powder and cook, stirring constantly, 30 seconds. Add cauliflower and stir.
3. Add tomatoes, coconut milk, and beans and mix well. Bring to boil and reduce heat. Cover and cook about 15 minutes, until mixture has thickened and cauliflower is tender.
4. Remove lid and add more salt and pepper if needed. Garnish with cilantro and serve.

Easy Saag Tofu

Saag paneer is a dish that comes from the Northern part of India. The words "saag" and "paneer" translate to "greens" and "cheese. The dish is traditionally made from spinach and includes lamb, but here is a vegetarian version that is very quick to make. Serve with warm naan bread.

Serves: 4-6
Time: 25 minutes
Ingredients:

- 1 pound extra-firm tofu, press for at least 15 minutes and cut into cubes
- 1 16-ounce bag frozen chopped spinach
- 2 cups canned diced tomatoes, undrained
- 1 medium yellow onion, chopped fine
- ¼ cup coconut milk
- ¼ cup water
- 5 tablespoons vegetable oil, divided
- 3 cloves garlic, chopped fine
- 1 tablespoon fresh ginger, chopped fine
- 2 teaspoons garam masala
- 1 teaspoon salt
- ½ teaspoon black pepper
- ¼ teaspoon cayenne pepper

Method:
1. Set cooker to sauté and add 4 tablespoons of oil. Once the oil is hot, add onion. Cook 4 minutes, then add tofu. Continue cooking, stirring gently so you don't break up the tofu, for 6-8 minutes or until onions and tofu begin to brown.
2. Add ginger and garlic and cook another 2 minutes. Add tofu, tomatoes, water, spinach, and seasonings. Stir gently to combine ingredients.
3. Close and lock lid. Select manual and set timer to 5 minutes.

4. When timer goes off, remove lid with quick release. Stir in the coconut milk and garam masala. Serve.

Faux Chow Mein

All the flavor of the Asian dish but none of the carbs. The spaghetti squash replaces the noodles in the dish for a lighter, healthier version.

Serves: 4
Time: 25 minutes
Ingredients:
- 1 large spaghetti squash, halved and seeds removed
- 1 cup water
- 2 cups coleslaw mix
- 3 stalks celery, sliced diagonally
- 1 onion, chopped fine
- ¼ cup tamari
- 3 cloves garlic, chopped fine
- 2 tablespoons olive oil
- 1 tablespoon sugar
- 2 teaspoons fresh ginger, grated
- ¼ teaspoon pepper

Method:
1. Place a trivet in the bottom of cooker. Add water and place squash on trivet. Close and lock lid. Select

manual setting and set timer to 6 minutes. When timer goes off, remove lid with quick release. Scoop out squash with a fork so it breaks apart; set aside.
2. Whisk together tamari, garlic, sugar, ginger, and pepper in a small bowl; set aside.
3. Set cooker to sauté and add oil. Once oil is hot, add onion and celery and cook 3-4 minutes, stirring frequently. Add coleslaw and cook just until heated through, about 1 minutes.
4. Add squash and sauce mixture and stir to combine. Cook, stirring frequently, about 2 minutes. Serve.

Gumbo

Gumbo is a rich stew traditionally made with chicken, sausage or seafood. This vegetarian style gumbo has all of the usual flavor of the ones you find in the South, just no meat! Perfect for those chilly winter nights. Serve over rice with cornbread or your favorite crusty bread for dipping.

Serves: 4-6
Time: 20 minutes
Ingredients:
- 2 cups vegetable broth
- 1 ½ cups tomatoes, diced
- 1 15-oz. can kidney beans, rinsed and drained well

- 1 green bell pepper, seeds and ribs removed and chopped
- 1 yellow onion, chopped
- 2 stalks celery, rinsed and chopped
- 1 small zucchini, sliced thick then cut into moons
- 1 cup white mushrooms, quartered
- 1 cup frozen sliced okra
- 3 cloves garlic, peeled and chopped fine
- 2 tablespoons olive oil
- 2 tablespoons all-purpose flour
- 2 tablespoons vegetarian Worcestershire sauce
- 1 tablespoon Cajun seasoning
- 1 bay leaf
- Salt and pepper, to taste

Method:
1. Set Instant Pot to Sauté and add 1 tablespoon of the oil; heat till hot. Add bell pepper, onion, celery, and garlic and cook till soft and not quite brown, about 5 minutes. Remove vegetables with slotted spoon and set aside.
2. Add the remaining tablespoon of oil to the pot. Add flour and cook, stirring constantly, till a roux has formed and turns a golden brown, about 4 minutes.
3. Add broth and heat to a boil. Add the reserved, cooked vegetables and the rest of the ingredients. Add lid and lock in place.

4. Set the pot to slow cooker function and the timer for 2 hours.
5. Release lid naturally and discard bay leaf. Add salt and pepper to taste. Serve.

Lentil Chili

A hearty bowl of chili and you won't even miss the meat! This healthier version of traditional chili meets many of the daily nutrients your body needs. Garnish with a dollop of sour cream and serve with warm tortillas.

Serves: 6-8

Time: 2 hours 10 minutes

Ingredients:
- 4 cups vegetable broth
- 1 ¾ cups water
- 1 15-oz. can tomato, diced
- 1 15-oz. can pinto beans, drained and rinsed
- 2 bell peppers, seeds and ribs removed and chopped
- 1 cup dried lentils
- 1 celery stalk, chopped
- 1 onion, chopped
- ½ cup quinoa, uncooked
- 3 garlic cloves, chopped fine
- 2 tablespoons chili powder
- 1 tablespoon oregano
- 2 teaspoons cumin

Method:
1. Add all ingredients to the inner pot of your cooker. Add lid and lock in place.

2. Set to slow cooker function and set the timer for 2 hours.
3. Release the lid naturally and serve.

Lightning Lo Mein

No need to call in that take-out order. This delicious Asian dish is packed with veggies and flavor that the whole family will love. You can have dinner on the table quicker than lightning, well almost!

Serves: 6
Time: 15 minutes
Ingredients:
- 3 cups broccoli florets
- 2 carrots, julienned
- 1 cup snow peas
- 1 5-ounce can sliced water chestnuts, drained
- 2 stalks celery, chopped
- 1 pound spaghetti noodles, cooked and drained well
- 1 cup water
- 1/3 cup soy sauce
- 3 cloves garlic, chopped fine
- 2 tablespoon brown sugar, packed
- 1 tablespoon oyster sauce
- 1 tablespoon ground fresh chili paste

- 1 tablespoon fresh ginger, grated
- 1 teaspoon sesame oil
- 1 teaspoon cornstarch

Method:
1. Place vegetables in inner pot of cooker.
2. In a small bowl, whisk together, water, soy sauce, garlic, brown sugar, oyster sauce, chili paste, ginger, sesame oil, and cornstarch. Add to vegetables and stir well.
3. Close and lock lid. Select manual and set timer for 3 minutes. When timer goes off, remove lid with quick release. Serve over cooked spaghetti.

Orange Tofu & Rice

5/2/18 tasty

Orange chicken is one of the most ordered dishes in Chinese restaurants. Now you can enjoy this vegetarian version at home! Serve over steamed rice and enjoy.

Serves: 4

Time: 2 hours

Ingredients:
- 1 package extra firm tofu, pressed for at least 15 minutes, cut into cubes
- 2 cups broccoli florets, fresh
- ¼ cup orange juice
- ¼ cup soy sauce

- ¼ cup honey
- 2 cloves garlic, chopped fine
- 1 tablespoon butter

Method:
1. Set cooker to sauté and add butter. Once butter is melted, add tofu and garlic. Cook, stirring occasionally, 5-10 minutes, or tofu begins to brown.
2. In a small bowl, whisk together wet ingredients.
3. Add broccoli and sauce to tofu and stir to mix.
4. Close and lock the lid. Select slow cooker function and set timer for 90 minutes. When timer goes off, remove lid with quick release and serve over rice.

Peanut Sauced Tofu

Peanut sauce dishes are traditional in Thai cooking. This take on Thai cuisine is not spicy, like most of their dishes are. By frying the tofu first, it will hold its shape and create a meaty texture. If you don't tell the family it's not chicken, they won't even know!

Serves: 4
Time: 90 minutes
Ingredients:
- 1 package of extra firm tofu, pressed 15 minutes and cut into cubes
- 1 package fresh baby spinach

- ½ cup peanut butter
- 2 limes
- 2 tablespoons soy sauce
- 1 tablespoon butter
- 3 cloves garlic, chopped fine
- ½ teaspoon ground ginger
- ¼ teaspoon crushed red pepper flakes

Method:
1. Set cooker to sauté and add butter. Once butter is melted, add tofu and garlic. Cook, stirring occasionally, 5-10 minutes or until tofu begins to brown.
2. Add remaining ingredients, except spinach and stir to combine. Close and lock lid. Select slow cooker and set timer for 60 minutes.
3. Use quick release to remove the lid. Add the spinach. Close and lock lid and set timer for 15 minutes. When timer goes off, use quick release again. Serve over rice or with stir fried vegetables.

Poblano & Zucchini Enchiladas

This layered enchilada dish is full of yummy flavors. With roasted poblano peppers and tomatillos, you get just the right amount of heat without setting your tongue on fire.

Serves: 4

Time: 70 mins

Ingredients:
- 10-12 corn tortillas
- 10 tomatillos
- 3 poblano peppers
- 2 zucchinis, sliced thin
- 1 cup Monterey Jack cheese, grated
- ½ cup mushrooms, sliced thin
- ¼ cup white onion, chopped fine
- ¼ cup cilantro, plus more for garnish
- 1 teaspoon salt

Method:
1. Place peppers on a cookie sheet and broil, 3 inches from burner, for 10-12 minutes. Turn peppers over and cook another 8-10 minutes, until charred. Put peppers in a paper bag, close tightly and let skins steam off. Let cool, then remove stems, seeds and skins.
2. Wash and husk tomatillos under warm water. Place on cookie sheet and broil, 10-12 minutes or until brown.
3. Place one pepper, tomatillos, cilantro, and salt in food processor. Process till smooth. Chop remaining peppers for casserole.
4. In a glass dish that will fit in your cooker, spread some of the tomatillo mix. Add layer of tortillas, then zucchini, mushrooms, and chopped pepper. Sprinkle

with some of the cheese. Repeat. End with layer of tortillas, tomatillos, and finally cheese.
5. Place a trivet in the bottom of your cooker and add 1 cup of water.
6. Cover casserole with foil and using a foil sling, lower into cooker. Close and lock lid. Select manual and set timer for 8 minutes. Use natural release to remove the lid. Serve garnished with sour cream and more chopped cilantro.

Quinoa Enchiladas

Mexican food is probably one of the most popular international cuisines existing. When you get a craving for something spicy and healthy, make a batch of these enchiladas. Hint—they are even better the next day for lunch!

Serves: 6-8
Time: 40 minutes
Ingredients:
- 4 cups butternut squash, peeled, seeded, and cut into small cubes
- 2 19-oz. cans mild red enchilada sauce
- 1 15.25-oz. can black beans, drained and rinsed well
- 1 14.5 oz. can fire-roasted tomatoes, diced
- 1 cup vegetable broth
- 1 cup quinoa, uncooked and rinsed

- 1 cup corn, frozen
- ¾ cup Monterey Jack cheese, grated
- 1 small jalapeno, seeded and chopped fine
- 10-12 corn tortillas
- 1 1.25-oz. package taco seasoning
- 1 clove garlic, peeled and chopped fine

Method:
1. Spray the inner pot with cooking spray. Add the vegetables, broth, 1 ½ cans enchilada sauce, and taco seasoning to pot. Add lid and lock in place. Cook on manual for 5 minutes.
2. Release lid and set to sauté. Allow to simmer until most of the liquid is absorbed, about 5 minutes.
3. Heat oven to 350 degrees. Place about ¼ cup of the mixture on a tortilla and roll up. Place in baking dish coated with cooking spray. Continue until all filling has been used.
4. Top with remaining enchilada sauce and sprinkle cheese over top. Bake until cheese has melted and starts to brown, about 20 – 25 minutes. Garnish as desired and serve.

Slow Cooked Stroganoff

Stroganoff is typically a rich dish made with beef and mushrooms. This version has most of the flavor without the beef. This recipe only serves 2, perfect for a single person with left overs. For a larger family, you will need to double it.

Serve over cooked rice or pasta with some toasty bread.

Serves; 2

Time: 2 hours 10 minutes

Ingredients:

- 8 cups mushrooms, cut into quarters
- 1 cup vegetable broth
- 3 cloves garlic, chopped fine
- 1 onion, cut in half and then sliced thin
- 4 tablespoons fresh parsley, chopped
- 1 ½ tablespoons sour cream
- 2 teaspoons smoked paprika
- Salt and pepper to taste

Method:

1. Add all ingredients, except sour cream and parsley, to cooker. Close and lock lid. Select slow cooker and set timer for 2 hours.
2. When timer goes off, use natural release to remove the lid. Stir in sour cream and serve, garnished with parsley.

Spaghetti & Lentil Meatballs

Spaghetti with meatballs for vegetarians? Yes, please! Meatballs made with lentils and mushrooms have the same texture as the ones made with ground beef. While this dish does take some time to prepare, the smiles on their faces will be worth it.

Serves: 4

Time: 60 minutes

Ingredients:

- 1 cup water
- 1 cup mushrooms
- ½ cup dried brown lentils, rinsed
- ½ cup vegetable broth
- ½ cup old-fashioned oats
- 2 cloves garlic, chopped fine
- 2 tablespoons red wine
- 1 tablespoon soy sauce
- 1 tablespoon olive oil
- 1 teaspoon Italian seasoning
- 1 bay leaf
- salt and pepper to taste

Method:

1. Set cooker to sauté. Add lentils, bay leaf and water. Bring to boil, then reduce heat. Cook 10 minutes.

Remove from pot and let cool slightly. Discard bay leaf.
2. Add lentils and mushrooms to food processor. Process till coarsely chopped.
3. Add olive oil to the cooker and heat. Once oil is hot, add garlic and sauté 30 seconds, stirring constantly. Add mushroom mixture and cook 4 minutes or until brown, stirring constantly.
4. Add wine and continue cooking till wine is evaporated. Stir in broth, soy sauce, oats, and seasoning. Cook until liquid is absorbed, stirring constantly. Remove from pot and season with salt and pepper. Let cool.
5. Heat oven to 350 degrees. Spray a mini muffin tin with cooking spray.
6. Shape the lentil mixture into 12 balls, placing each in cup of prepared tin. Bake 40 minutes, or until nicely browned.
7. Serve over cooked spaghetti noodles with your favorite sauce.

Stuffed Red Peppers

This dish is extremely easy and very versatile. Many leftover vegetables may be added to the rice for stuffing the peppers. For the recipe, I used a leftover Mexican dish I had in the refrigerator made from lentils, corn and salsa.

Serves: 4   **Time**: 2 hours

Ingredients:

- 4 red bell peppers (look for flat bottoms)
- 1 cup brown rice, cooked
- ½ cup lentils, cooked
- ½ cup corn, frozen
- ½ cup salsa
- ½ cup cheddar cheese, grated
- 1/3 cup water

Method:

1. Cut ½ inch off the tops of the peppers and dice the tops.
2. In a medium bowl, combine rice, lentils, corn, salsa, and diced peppers.
3. Stuff the peppers with the rice mixture and sit upright on the bottom of the cooker.
4. Add the water around the peppers. Close and lock the lid. Select slow cooker function and set the timer to 90

minutes. When timer goes off, remove lid with the natural release setting.
5. Sprinkle tops of peppers with cheese and cover until cheese melts. Serve.

Super Simple Mac 'N Cheese

Homemade mac 'n cheese in 20 minutes, with uncooked pasta! Yes, it can be done. Enjoy everyone's favorite comfort food with no muss and no fuss!

Serves: 8
Time: 20 minutes
Ingredients:
- 1 pound macaroni
- 2 cups half and half
- 2 cups cheddar cheese, grated
- 1 cup water
- 2 tablespoons butter
- ½ teaspoon salt

Method:
1. Set cooker to sauté and add butter. When butter has melted, add macaroni and water.
2. Cook, stirring constantly, until water is almost gone. Add remaining ingredients, reserving ½ cup of the cheese, and stir well.

3. Close and lock lid. Select manual function and set timer to 10 minutes. When timer goes off, use quick release to remove lid. Sprinkle with reserved cheese and cover until it melts. Serve.

Sweet Potato Pasta with Cashew Sauce

Creamy spinach on top of sweet potato noodles covered in a cashew sauce! Easy to make, adaptable, and gluten free. Deliciously divine!

Serves: 5
Time: 50 minutes
Ingredients:

- 4 large sweet potatoes, cut with spiral cutter
- 2 cups baby spinach
- 1 cup cashews, soaked in water for 2 hours, drained and rinsed
- ¾ cup water (more for soaking)
- ½ cup fresh basil, coarsely chopped
- 1 clove garlic
- 1 tablespoon olive oil
- ½ teaspoon salt

Method:

1. Place cashews, water, salt, and garlic in a food processor. Puree until smooth.

2. Set cooker to sauté and add oil. Once oil is hot, add sweet potatoes and cook, 6-7 minutes, tossing frequently, until tender-crisp. Remove from heat.
3. Add spinach to the pot and cook until wilted, about 2 minutes. Add half the basil and the sauce and stir to combine. If the sauce is too sticky, add more water, in small amounts.
4. To serve, place sweet potatoes on serving plate and top with cashew sauce. Lightly drizzle with olive oil and garnish with remaining basil leaves.

Tofu Curry

Curry is spice that adds heat and flavor to your dishes. It is used in a lot of Indian cuisine. If you like heat, nothing beats a good curry like this vegetarian option, using tofu in place of the usual lamb or chicken.

Serves: 4
Time: 2 hours 10 minutes
Ingredients:

- 2 cups green bell pepper, ribs and seeds removed and cut into chunks
- 1 cup firm tofu, chopped
- 1 ½ cups canned coconut milk
- 1 cup tomato paste

- 1 small onion, peeled and chopped
- 2 cloves garlic, peeled and chopped fine
- 2 tablespoons peanut butter
- 1 tablespoon Garam Masala
- 1 tablespoon curry powder
- 1 ½ teaspoons sea salt

Method:
1. Spray inner pot of cooker with cooking spray.
2. Add all ingredients, except the tofu, to a blender or food processor. Process until thoroughly combined.
3. Pour into the prepared inner pot and add the tofu. Add lid and lock into place. Select slow cooker function and set timer to 2 hours.
4. Release the lid and serve over cooked rice if desired.

Tomato & Spinach Frittata

A frittata is similar to a quiche but without the pie crust. It's a simple dish to prepare and light enough that you can still go out afterward! Makes the ideal summer meal served with a tossed green salad.

Serves: 6
Time: 50 mins
Ingredients:
- 1 dozen large eggs
- 3 cups fresh baby spinach, roughly chopped

- 1 cup tomato, seeds removed and chopped
- 3 large green onions, sliced
- 4 tomato slices
- ½ cup milk
- ¼ cup Parmesan cheese, grated
- ½ teaspoon salt
- ¼ teaspoon pepper

Method:
1. Place a trivet on the bottom of the cooker and add 1 ½ cups water.
2. Whisk eggs, milk, salt, and pepper in a large mixing bowl.
3. Put spinach, chopped tomatoes, and onions in a glass baking dish and toss to combine. Pour eggs over vegetables and stir to combine. Place sliced tomatoes on top and sprinkle with parmesan cheese.
4. Use a foil sling to place the baking dish on trivet. Close and lock the lid. Select high pressure and set timer for 20 minutes. When timer goes off, use natural release to remove the lid. Use the foil sling to remove the baking dish, and serve.

Winter Squash Lasagna

This Italian comfort food gets an upgrade. Instead of the usual tomato sauce, this recipe uses winter squash to create a new, sophisticated version of everyone's favorite. Serve with a crisp, green salad and toasted garlic bread.

Serves: 6

Time: 2 hours 10 minutes

Ingredients:

- 6 cups baby spinach
- 2 ½ cups frozen winter squash, thawed
- 1 32-oz. container ricotta cheese
- 12 lasagna noodles
- 1 cup mozzarella cheese, grated
- 1/8 teaspoon nutmeg
- Salt and pepper to taste

Method:

1. Spray the inner pot of your cooker with cooking spray.
2. In a medium bowl, mix the squash and nutmeg.
3. In a separate bowl, mix ricotta, spinach, ½ teaspoon salt, and ¼ teaspoon pepper.
4. Spread ½ cup of the squash in bottom of prepared pot. Top with layer of noodles, breaking to fit. Add ½ the remaining squash mixture, another layer of noodles, and ½ the ricotta mixture. Repeat, being sure to end with the ricotta mix. Sprinkle mozzarella over top.
5. Add lid and lock into place. Select the slow cooker function and set timer to 2 hours.
6. Release lid naturally and serve.

Side Dishes

Apple Sage Stuffing

Apple and sage come together in this delicious holiday dish. It's so good even the meat eaters will ask for more! Use it to stuff the turkey or serve it alongside.

Serves: 4

Time: 3 hours 20 minutes

Ingredients:

- 2 cups of mushrooms, sliced
- 2 sweet potatoes, peeled and chopped
- 1 Granny Smith apple, peeled, cored, and diced
- ¾ cup celery, chopped
- ½ yellow onion, chopped fine
- ½ cup pecans, chopped
- 9 fresh sage leaves, chopped fine and divided
- ¼ cup dried cranberries
- ¼ cup vegetable broth
- 3 cloves of garlic, chopped fine
- 2 tablespoons butter, melted
- Salt and pepper to taste

Method:

1. Add all the dry ingredients to the cooker. Pour butter over and mix. Salt and pepper to taste. Add broth and mix again.

2. Close and lock lid. Select slow cooker function and set timer for 3 hours. When timer goes off, remove lid with natural release. Salt and pepper to taste and serve.

Austrian Stewed Cabbage

When sour kraut just won't do, and you've run out of ideas for a quick, healthy side dish, make a batch of this stewed cabbage. The flavor comes from the beer, so be sure to use a good quality. You can use a pale ale if you prefer.

Serves: 4

Time: 18 minutes

Ingredients:
- 1 medium savoy cabbage, cut into strips
- 1 medium onion, cut into strips
- 1 cup beer or pale ale
- 1 tablespoon butter

Method:
1. Wash and dry the cut cabbage.
2. Set cooker to sauté and add butter and onion. Cook, stirring occasionally, about 5 minutes or until onions start to get soft.
3. Add cabbage and beer. Close and lock lid. Select manual function and set the timer for 3 minutes.
4. When the timer goes off, remove the lid using quick release. Stir and serve.

Basic Risotto

This basic risotto is good as is, or feel free to experiment by adding other ingredients. To give you some ideas, mushrooms work well; try some cilantro and lime or whatever you like!

Serves: 4
Time: 25 minutes
Ingredients:

- 2 ½ cups hot vegetable broth
- 1 ⅓ cups Arborio rice
- 1 medium onion, chopped fine
- ⅓ cup dry white wine
- 3 tablespoons Parmesan cheese, grated
- 1 tablespoon olive oil
- 1 tablespoon sweet butter

Method:

1. Set cooker to sauté and add oil. Once oil is hot, add onions and cook, stirring occasionally, about 5 minutes or until they become translucent. Add rice and cook 1 minute more.
2. Add wine and cook, stirring constantly, until it is mostly absorbed.
3. Add the broth and mix well. Close and lock the lid. Select manual function and set timer for 6 minutes.

When the timer goes off, use quick release to remove the lid.
4. Select sauté again and bring rice to simmer. Whisk in butter and cheese, and if you are adding additional items, do it at this step. Cook, stirring constantly, about 1 minute, then cover.
5. Turn the cooker off and let risotto rest 3-5 minutes. Serve.

Brussel Sprouts with Parmesan

Brussel sprouts may be one of the least popular vegetables, but these little beauties are so good for the body, rich in vitamins C and B6, nutrients such as manganese and calcium, and they are high in iron. So, try this quick and easy recipe for a healthy side at dinner.

Serves: 4

Time: 15 minutes

Ingredients:
- 1 lb. Brussel sprouts, washed and trimmed
- 1 cup water
- 1 lemon
- 2 tablespoons butter
- Fresh Parmesan cheese, grated

Method:
1. Preheat the cooker by selecting the sauté function.

2. Add water to the pot. Place the Brussel sprouts in the steamer basket and add to pot.
3. Close and lock lid. Set the cooker to manual and the timer to 2 minutes. When the timer goes off, use quick release to remove the lid. Lift sprouts out and discard the water.
4. Set the cooker back to sauté and add the butter, juice from lemon and the sprouts. Cook, stirring frequently, until sprouts turn a golden brown. Transfer to serving dish and sprinkle with cheese.

Cheesy Broccoli Casserole

One of my favorite sides, I could eat this almost every day of the week. This casserole is so easy to make that it is a great time saver for busy moms. You can switch it up by replacing the broccoli with cauliflower, too. And with all of the cheesy goodness, the kids will love it!

Serves: 8-10

Time: 2 hours 35 minutes

Ingredients:

- 2 packages frozen broccoli, chopped and almost thawed
- 1 ½ cups cheddar cheese, grated
- 1 can condensed cream of celery soup
- 1 cup butter-flavor crackers, crushed

- ¼ cup yellow onion, chopped fine
- 2 tablespoons butter, cut into small pieces
- ½ teaspoon vegan Worcestershire sauce
- ¼ teaspoon pepper

Method:
1. In a large mixing bowl, stir together broccoli, soup, 1 cup of cheese, onions, Worcestershire sauce, and pepper.
2. Spray the inner pot of cooker with cooking spray. Add the broccoli to the pot. Sprinkle the cracker crumbs evenly over the top. Add the butter pieces over the top.
3. Close and lock lid. Select slow cooker function and set timer for 2 ½ hours. When timer goes off, remove the lid with quick release.
4. Sprinkle remaining cheese over top and cover until cheese melts, about 5-10 minutes. Serve.

Creamy BBQ Cauliflower

A new twist on cauliflower. If your kids like anything BBQ, like mine, they are going to like this. An ideal dish for summertime and backyard barbecues.

Serves: 4
Time: 15 minutes
Ingredients:
- 1 head cauliflower; trim the bottom

- 2/3 cup BBQ sauce, plus extra
- ½ cup vegetable broth
- ½ cup pecans, coarsely chopped
- 4 tablespoons butter, melted
- 3 tablespoons blue cheese, crumbled

Method:
1. In a small bowl, whisk together BBQ sauce and butter. Brush over the cauliflower.
2. Place the cauliflower in the cooker and pour the broth around it. Close and lock lid. Select manual function and set timer for 4 minutes. When timer goes off, remove the lid using quick release function.
3. Preheat the broiler. Remove cauliflower and separate into florets. Place the florets on a baking sheet, in single layer. Brush with BBQ sauce and broil 3-5 minutes, or brown. Serve immediately, garnished with blue cheese and pecans.

Easy Cheesy Cauliflower

What goes better with cauliflower than melted cheese? This dish is a bit different in that it calls for Mozzarella instead of the usual cheddar. Even better, it only takes 10 minutes or less to prepare!

Serves: 6
Time: 10 minutes

Ingredients:
- 2 lbs. cauliflower, separated into florets
- 2 cups milk
- 1 ½ cups mozzarella, grated
- ¼ cup flour
- ¼ cup butter
- ½ teaspoon salt
- ¼ teaspoon black pepper

Method:
1. Set cooker to sauté. Add butter and melt. Stir in flour and seasonings, mix well. Add the milk and cook, stirring constantly, until sauce thickens and begins to bubble, about 5 minutes. Press cancel and add the cheese. Stir until smooth.
2. Add the cauliflower and stir to combine. Close and lock lid. Select manual function and set timer for 2 minutes. When timer goes off, remove lid with quick release option. Serve.

Easy Corn Soufflé

This tasty soufflé is a cross between cornbread and corn pudding. The texture meets somewhere in the middle. Makes a great side dish for holiday dinners when you want to wow your family and friends.

Serves: 6

Time: 2 hours 25 minutes

Ingredients:
- 1 ½ cups fresh corn kernels
- 1 can cream corn
- 1 package corn muffin mix
- ½ cup sour cream
- 1/3 cup green onions, just the green ends, chopped
- 6 tablespoons butter, melted

Method:
1. In a large bowl, combine all ingredients. Stir to mix well.
2. Spray the inner pot of cooker with cooking spray. Add the soufflé to the pot.
3. Close and lock lid. Select slow cooker function and set timer to 2 hours. When timer goes off, remove lid with natural release function. Let soufflé rest about 20 minutes before serving.

Fried Cabbage & Rice

Another great dish that offers a new way to serve cabbage. This Indian inspired recipe has tons of flavor. Ginger and garam masala give it that Indian taste while the cashews add a nice crunch.

Serves: 4
Time: 30 minutes

Ingredients:
- 4 tomatoes, seeded and cut into fourths
- 1 cup cabbage, shredded, rinsed and dried
- 1 cup green peas
- 1 cup basmati rice
- 1 cup water
- 1 onions, peeled and chopped
- 5 green chilies, seeds and ribs removed
- 1/3 cup cashew nuts
- 20 cloves garlic, peeled
- 10 tablespoons olive oil
- 2 tablespoons fresh ginger, grated
- 1 tablespoon garam masala
- 1 tablespoon butter

Method:
1. Set cooker to sauté and add 3-4 tablespoons oil. When the oil is hot, add cabbage. Cook, stirring frequently, about 5-8 minutes or until it is nicely browned. Remove from pot and set aside.
2. Add tomatoes, garlic, ginger, onion, and chilies to a food processor. Process until the mixture forms a smooth paste.
3. Add 1-2 tablespoons oil and butter to cooker and melt the butter. Then add cashews and garam masala. Cook,

stirring frequently, until cashews start to brown. Add tomato paste and cook another 2-3 minutes.
4. Add the peas and cook 4 minutes or until peas are tender. Add rice, water, and cabbage; stir to mix.
5. Close and lock lid. Select manual function and set timer to 5 minutes. Remove lid with natural release. Serve.

Italian Red Potatoes

Quick and easy dish that has the flavors of roasted potatoes without the time it takes to roast them! Add Italian seasoning and parmesan cheese, and you have a home run!

Serves: 4
Time: 15 minutes
Ingredients:
- 5-6 red potatoes, cut into fourths
- 1 cup vegetable broth
- ½ cup parmesan cheese, grated
- 2 tablespoons butter
- 2 teaspoons Italian seasoning
- Coarse sea salt

Method:
1. Set cooker to sauté and add butter. Once butter is melted, add potatoes. Cook, stirring occasionally, until potatoes start to brown.

2. Add broth and Italian seasoning. Close and lock lid. Select manual function and set timer for 5 minutes.
3. When timer goes off, remove lid using quick release. Transfer potatoes to serving dish and sprinkle with cheese and salt.

Maple Glazed Carrots

Sweet, delicious, and good for you too! These make an ideal dish for the holidays or Sunday dinner, and they taste like you spent a lot of time making them.

Serves: 4

Time: 25 minutes

Ingredients:
- 3 lbs. carrots, peeled and cut in fourths lengthwise
- 2 tablespoons vegetable broth
- 1 tablespoon butter
- 1 tablespoon whole grain mustard
- 1 tablespoon maple syrup
- 1 teaspoon thyme
- ¼ teaspoon baking soda

Method:
1. Set cooker to sauté and add butter. Once butter melts, add all ingredients except carrots. Stir well.
2. Add carrots and stir to coat. Close and lock lid. Select manual function and set timer for 4 minutes.

3. When timer goes off, remove lid using natural release function. Stir and serve.

Sweet Potato & Apple Casserole

This casserole makes a nice alternative to the traditional sweet potatoes served for the holidays, and it is lower in calories, quicker to make, and healthier too!

Serves: 8   **Time**: 15 minutes

Ingredients:
- 5 medium sweet potatoes, peeled and cut into 1-inch cubes
- 2 Granny Smith apples, peeled, seeded and chopped
- ½ cup water
- ½ cup milk
- ½ cup pecans, coarsely chopped and lightly toasted
- ¼ cup honey
- 2 tablespoons unsalted butter
- 2 teaspoons cinnamon
- ¼ teaspoon nutmeg
- ½ teaspoon salt

Method:
1. Add all ingredients, except milk, pecans, and butter, to the cooker. Stir to combine.

2. Close and lock lid. Select manual function and set timer to 4 minutes. When timer goes off, remove lid with natural release.
3. Use a potato masher and mash to desired consistency. Add milk and butter and mix well. Top with pecans and serve.

Sweet Potato Risotto

Rich, creamy risotto packed with nutrients. Sweet potatoes are one of nature's superfoods and contain many essential nutrients, vitamins A and C, and most of the B's. This dish ensures you get more of these in your diet because you will want to make it again and again!

Serves: 4
Time: 30 minutes
Ingredients:
- 4 ½ cups vegetable broth
- 2 sweet potatoes, baked, skins removed and chopped
- 2 cups Arborio rice
- 1 cup porcini mushrooms, rinsed and dried
- 1 cup Fontina cheese, grated
- 4 shallots, chopped fine
- ¼ cup white wine
- 4 cloves garlic, chopped fine

- 2 teaspoons olive oil
- Salt and pepper to taste
- Cayenne pepper and toasted pine nuts, for garnish

Method:
1. Set cooker to sauté and add oil, onion and garlic. Cook, stirring frequently, until soft, about 4-5 minutes. Add rice and cook another 2 minutes.
2. Add wine and continue cooking until most of the wine evaporates. Add broth, potatoes, and mushrooms. Close and lock the lid. Select manual function and set timer for 7 minutes.
3. When timer goes off, use the quick release to remove lid. Stir in cheese, salt, pepper, and cayenne if desired. Serve garnished with pine nuts and more cheese.

Zucchini Fritters with Garlic Dipping Sauce

Picky eaters, meaning kids, love anything they can dip. One way to get more vegetables in them is by making these fritters. Most of the ingredients you probably have in the kitchen already. They make a great lunch or after school snack too!

Serves: 4
Time: 40 minutes
Ingredients:

- 3 medium zucchinis, grated
- 1 onion, chopped
- ¾ cup feta cheese, crumbled
- ½ cup flour
- 2 eggs
- ¼ cup fresh dill, chopped
- 1 tablespoon butter
- 1 teaspoon salt
- Pepper to taste
- Oil for frying

Garlic Yogurt Sauce:
- 1 cup Greek yogurt
- 1 tablespoon fresh dill, chopped fine
- 2 cloves garlic, chopped fine

Method:
1. Place zucchini in a large colander and sprinkle with the salt. Toss with fingers and let sit 30 minutes. Squeeze with back of spoon to remove the excess water. Place the zucchini between paper towels and squeeze again. Place in large bowl and let dry.
2. Set cooker to sauté and add butter. Once butter has melted, add onion and cook about 5 minutes or until onion starts to get soft. Remove from cooker and add to zucchini along with the cheese and dill and combine thoroughly.

3. In a small bowl, whisk together the flour and eggs. Pour over zucchini and mix well.
4. Add enough oil to the cooker to equal ½ inch on the bottom and let heat until it is very hot. Drop the zucchini mixture into oil, about the size of a golf ball, and flatten into patty. Cook until nicely browned on both sides. Remove from oil and drain on paper towels.
5. Stir the dipping sauce ingredients together in a small bowl. Serve.

Soups & Stews

African Spicy Peanut Stew

This hearty stew is inspired by African recipes. The sweet potatoes and peanut butter give it a richness that warms the belly and the heart.

Servings: 6-8
Time: 25 minutes
Ingredients:

- 2 ¼ pounds sweet potatoes, peeled and cut into 1-inch pieces
- 2 14.5-ounce cans chickpeas, drained and rinsed
- 2 14.5-ounce cans tomatoes, diced
- 1 pound green beans, cut in 1-inch pieces
- 1 ½ cups vegetable broth

- 1 onion, chopped
- ¼ cup peanut butter
- 2 jalapenos, seeds and ribs removed and chopped fine
- 2 tablespoons water
- 2 teaspoons ground cumin
- 2 teaspoons fresh ginger, chopped fine
- 1 teaspoon garlic, chopped fine
- ½ teaspoon salt
- ¼ teaspoon ground coriander
- ¼ teaspoon ground cinnamon
- 1/8 teaspoon red pepper flakes

Method:
1. Set cooker to sauté and add water, onion, and jalapenos. Cook, stirring occasionally, about 8 minutes or till vegetables are soft. Stir in spices and cook 1 minute more, stirring constantly.
2. Add sweet potatoes, chickpeas, tomatoes with their liquid, and broth. Close and lock lid. Select manual function and set timer for 5 minutes. When timer goes off, remove lid with quick release.
3. Add green beans and peanut butter. Close and lock lid and set timer for 1 minute. Use quick release again when timer goes off. Stir well and serve.

Asparagus Lemon Bisque

A lovely soup for spring and summer. Asparagus is easy to find, and the lemon brightens the flavors. Just a few minutes are spent making this soup, so you won't heat up the kitchen.

Serves: 4

Time: 20 mins

Ingredients:

- 2 pounds fresh asparagus; remove the bottom 1/3 and cut into small pieces
- 4 cups vegetable broth
- 1 yellow onion, chopped
- 1 small lemon, zest and juice
- 3 tablespoons olive oil
- 3 cloves garlic, chopped fine
- 1 teaspoon fresh thyme, chopped fine
- salt and pepper, to taste

Method:

1. Set cooker to sauté and add oil. Once oil is hot, add asparagus and onion and cook, stirring occasionally, 5 minutes or until nicely browned. Add garlic and cook another minute.
2. Add remaining ingredients and stir to combine. Close and lock lid. Select manual function and set timer for 5

minutes. When timer goes off, use quick release to remove lid.
3. Use an immersion blender, or transfer to blender, and blend until the soup is smooth. Salt and pepper to taste and serve.

Autumn Veggie Stew

This delicious stew uses the best of the autumn harvest. Leeks, carrots, peas, and lentils combine to create the perfect bowl of stew for those chilly nights. Serve garnished with fresh parsley and a squeeze of lemon juice.

Serves: 4-6
Time: 20 minutes
Ingredients:
- 3 cups chopped celery root
- 1 ½ cups vegetable broth
- 1 cup parsnip, chopped
- 1 cup leek, sliced
- 1 cup carrot, chopped
- ½ cup French green lentils
- ½ cup fresh or frozen peas
- 3 cloves garlic, chopped fine
- 2 bay leaves
- 1 to 2 sprigs thyme

- 1 sprig rosemary
- Salt and pepper, to taste

Method:
1. Set cooker to sauté and add the leek. Dry sauté for 1 minute. Add garlic and cook for 1 minute more, stirring frequently.
2. Add remaining ingredients, except the peas. Close and lock lid. Select manual setting and set timer for 6 minutes. When timer goes off, use natural release to open the lid.
3. Add peas, stir, and close and lock the lid. Set timer for 2 minutes. Use quick release to remove the lid. Discard herbs, and salt and pepper to taste. Serve.

Carrot Cashew Bisque

This nutty, almost sweet soup makes a great dinner. Best made in the summer when corn is at its peak. Serve this one warm or cold; either way, it's delicious.

Serves: 4-6
Time: 50 minutes
Ingredients:
- 6 cups vegetable broth
- 3 cups fresh corn kernels
- 3 carrots, chopped
- 2 white onions, chopped

- 1 cup cashews, roasted
- 4 tablespoons butter
- ¼ teaspoon baking soda

Method:
1. Set cooker to sauté and add butter. Once butter has melted, add onions, carrots, and cashews. Cook, stirring occasionally, about 5 minutes.
2. Add the broth, corn, and baking soda. Close and lock lid. Select manual setting and set timer for 20 minutes.
3. When timer goes off, remove lid with quick release. Use an immersion blender or transfer to blender and process until smooth. Serve warm or cold.

Cheesy Spinach Bisque

Nothing feels better at the end of a long day than curling up in your favorite pj's with a good book. Well, this soup feels a lot like that—pure bliss! This is really tasty served in a bread bowl!

Serves: 8
Time: 90 minutes
Ingredients:
- 1 lb. Velveeta cheese, cut into cubes
- 2 cups milk
- 1 package frozen spinach, chopped, thawed, and drained

- 1 cup water
- ½ cup onion, chopped
- ¼ cup flour
- ¼ cup butter, melted
- ½ teaspoon sea salt
- ¼ teaspoon ground nutmeg

Method:
1. In a medium mixing bowl, whisk together butter and flour to form a roux. Slowly whisk in milk and water. Add salt and nutmeg.
2. Place the cheese, spinach and onion in the cooker. Pour in milk mixture. Close and lock lid. Select the slow cooker function and set timer for 90 minutes. Remove lid with natural release function. Stir well before serving.

Creamy Cauliflower & Sweet Potato Bisque

Two superfoods packed into one yummy soup. I love the creamy texture of bisques, and they are usually better the next day after the flavors have had time to blend. This one makes a great meal any time of year. Serve topped with a slice of avocado.

Serves: 4

Time: 15 minutes

Ingredients:
- 1 head cauliflower, separated into large florets
- 1 large sweet potato, peeled and cut into cubes
- 1 onion, chopped fine
- 2 cups vegetable broth
- 1 cup milk
- 1/3 block of cream cheese, cut into cubes
- 2 cloves garlic, peeled
- ½ teaspoon rosemary
- 1/8 teaspoon red pepper flakes
- Salt and pepper to taste

Method:
1. Place vegetables, broth, and seasonings in cooker. Close and lock lid. Select manual setting and set timer for 5 minutes. When timer goes off, remove lid with natural release option.
2. Add milk and cream cheese. Use an immersion blender, or transfer to blender, and process until smooth. Salt and pepper to taste and serve.

Enchilada Soup

All the flavor of chicken enchiladas, minus the chicken, of course. This soup has just the right amount of heat and is easy to put together. Serve topped with your favorite toppings like sour cream, chopped fresh cilantro, cheddar cheese or sliced avocado!

Serves: 6

Time: 10 minutes

Ingredients:
- 1 can black beans, rinsed and drained
- 1 can petite tomatoes, diced
- 3 cups vegetable broth
- 2 cups corn, frozen
- 1 small can tomato sauce
- ½ cup onion, chopped
- ¼ cup cilantro, chopped
- 3 cloves garlic, chopped fine
- 2 teaspoon olive oil
- 1-2 teaspoon chipotle chili in adobo sauce
- 1 teaspoon cumin
- ½ teaspoon oregano

Method:
1. Set cooker to sauté and add oil. When oil is hot, add onion and garlic, cook 3-4 minutes until soft. Slowly pour in broth; stir to combine. Add remaining ingredients and stir to combine.
2. Close and lock lid. Select manual setting and set timer for 20 minutes. When timer goes off, remove lid with quick release. Serve with your favorite toppings.

Hearty Barley Stew

This one is at the top of my list of wintertime comfort foods. I love a rich bowl of soup filled with barley, carrots, and potatoes. The vitamins and nutrients packed into this stew work almost as well as Grandma's chicken soup when you are feeling under the weather.

Serves: 6
Time: 45 minutes
Ingredients:
- 3 large carrots, peeled and cut into ½ inch thick slices
- 1 28-oz. can crushed tomatoes
- 2 ½ cups water
- 1 large potato, peeled and chopped
- 2 stalks celery, chopped
- 1 medium onion, chopped
- ½ cup barley
- 1 clove garlic, chopped fine
- ½ teaspoon each basil, thyme, marjoram, rosemary
- ¼ teaspoon salt

Method:
1. Put tomatoes, water, and barley in the cooker. Close and lock lid. Select manual setting and set timer for 10 minutes.

2. When timer goes off, use quick release to open the lid. Add remaining ingredients. Close and lock lid again. Set timer for 10 minutes more. When timer goes off, release pressure and remove lid. Stir well and serve.

Pumpkin Lentil Stew

In the fall, when everything is pumpkin flavored, why not soup too? This low calorie, healthy soup is ideal served on a chilly fall day. Since it's so quick to make, you can throw it together easily after a long day. If you prefer, you can substitute butternut squash for the pumpkin.

Serves: 6
Time: 25 minutes
Ingredients:
- 2 lbs. pumpkin, cut into bite sized pieces
- 4 cups fat-free vegetable broth
- 1 large onion, chopped fine
- 1 cup green lentils
- ½ cup plain Greek yogurt
- 2 tablespoons tomato paste
- 1 tablespoon ground ginger
- 1 tablespoon cumin
- 1 lime, juiced
- 1 teaspoon salt

- 1 teaspoon nutmeg
- 1 teaspoon turmeric
- ½ teaspoon black pepper
- Cilantro, chopped for garnish

Method:
1. Place all ingredients, except yogurt and cilantro, in the cooker. Close and lock lid. Select manual setting and set timer for 10 minutes.
2. When timer goes off, remove lid with natural release option. Serve topped with a tablespoon of yogurt and pinch of cilantro.

Spicy Carrot & Sweet Potato Soup

Perfect soup for those chilly winter nights. Made from harvest vegetables and spices that not only add healthy benefits to the soup but pack it with flavor.

Serves: 4
Time: 20 minutes
Ingredients:
- 1 ¾ cups coconut milk
- 1 cup vegetable stock
- 6 medium carrots (peeled and chopped small)
- 1 small yellow onion (minced)
- 1 large sweet potato (peeled and chopped small)

- 1 tablespoon olive oil
- 1 ½ teaspoon salt
- ½ teaspoon chili powder
- ½ teaspoon turmeric
- ½ teaspoon cinnamon
- ½ teaspoon cumin
- ¼ teaspoon smoked paprika

Method:
1. Peel and chop the vegetables.
2. Set your Instant Pot to Sauté and keep the temperature at normal. Add olive oil and heat until hot. Add the vegetables and cook, stirring occasionally, 4-5 minutes.
3. Add remaining ingredients, except coconut milk, and stir to mix well. Cook on high pressure for 5 minutes.
4. Release the pressure and add the coconut milk.
5. Use an immersion blender, or transfer to regular blender, and puree soup until smooth.
6. Garnish with roasted pumpkin seeds, if desired, and serve immediately.

Spicy Chickpea & Tomato Stew

Hearty chickpeas, spinach, and tomatoes with just enough heat to keep your tongue awake. This soup packs in plenty of vitamins and nutrients to give your body the fuel it needs.

Makes a great lunch time meal to keep you going the rest of the day! Or, serve over steamed rice for a filling dinner.

Serves: 6

Time: 20 minutes

Ingredients:
- 2 cups dried chickpeas, cooked and drained
- 2 cups tomatoes, chopped
- 2 cups baby spinach leaves
- 2 onions, chopped fine
- 2 tablespoons fresh ginger, chopped fine
- 4 cloves garlic, chopped fine
- 1 tablespoon olive oil
- 2 teaspoons balsamic vinegar
- 2 teaspoons coriander, ground
- 1 teaspoon coriander seeds
- 1 teaspoon salt
- ½ teaspoon pepper

Method:
1. Set cooker to sauté and add oil. When oil is hot, add onions and cook, stirring frequently, till onions begin to brown, about 5-6 minutes. Add remaining spices and cook 1 minute more.
2. Add vinegar and tomatoes. Bring to a boil; switch to manual setting.

3. Add chickpeas. Close and lock lid. Set timer to 10 minutes. When timer goes off, use quick release to remove the lid.
4. Add spinach and stir well. Serve.

Split Second Split Pea Soup

This is a popular soup traditionally made with ham, but who needs the ham? This soup is just as flavorful without it and, like most of the recipes here, quick and easy to prepare. Who doesn't love quick and easy—or inexpensive? This whole pot of soup can be made for less than $5!

Serves: 6
Time: 20 minutes
Ingredients:
- 1 lb. split peas
- 6 cups vegetable broth
- 3 carrots, sliced
- 3 stalks celery, sliced
- 1 yellow onion, chopped fine
- 2 tablespoons coconut oil
- 2 cloves garlic, chopped fine
- ½ tablespoon paprika
- 1 bay leaf
- ½ teaspoon thyme

- salt and pepper

Method:
1. Place all ingredients in cooker. Close and lock the lid. Select manual setting and set timer for 15 minutes.
2. When timer goes off, remove lid with natural release option. Stir well. Add salt and pepper to taste and serve.

Sweet Corn Chowder

This chowder is a perfect summer meal. Corn is at its sweetest, and cooking it won't heat up the kitchen! You can substitute milk for the half-n-half but I think the texture is creamier without milk.

Serves: 6-8
Time: 35 minutes
Ingredients:
- 6 ears sweet corn; remove kernels but do not discard cobs
- 2 potatoes, chopped
- 3 cups half-and-half
- 3 cups + 2 tablespoons water
- ½ cup onion, chopped
- 4 tablespoons butter
- 2 tablespoons cornstarch

- 2 tablespoons fresh parsley, chopped
- 1/8 teaspoon cayenne pepper
- Salt and pepper to taste

Method:
1. Set cooker to sauté and add butter. Once butter has melted, add onion and cook, stirring occasionally, about 3 minutes or until onion is tender.
2. Add 3 cups water and corncobs. Close and lock lid. Select manual setting and set timer for 10 minutes. When timer goes off, remove lid with quick release. Remove cobs and discard.
3. Place the steamer basket in pot. Add potatoes and corn. Close and lock lid. Set timer for 4 minutes. When timer goes off, do quick release again. Remove basket of vegetables carefully.
4. In a small bowl, whisk together cornstarch and 2 tablespoons of water. Select sauté again and add cornstarch mixture to pot. Cook and stir constantly until soup begins to thicken.
5. Stir in half-n-half, corn, potatoes, parsley, and cayenne pepper. Add salt and pepper to taste. Continue cooking and stirring just until chowder is heated through; do not boil. Serve warm.

Tipsy Onion Soup

Don't let the name fool you, this soup is perfectly safe for folks under 21! This rich onion soup has just a little twist, beer. Use a good quality dark beer to enhance all the flavors. Serve with toasted French bread, covered in melted cheese—yum!

Serves: 8-12
Time: 4 hours
Ingredients:

- 6 cups yellow onions, thinly sliced
- 4 cups vegetable broth
- 3 cups dark beer
- 1 cup potatoes, chopped small
- ½ cup celery, chopped fine
- 4 tablespoons olive oil
- ½ cup flour
- 2 tablespoons water
- 2 tablespoons butter
- 4 cloves garlic, chopped fine

Method:

1. Place onions in cooker. Add water and drizzle with 4 tablespoons oil. Close and lock lid. Select slow cooker function and set timer for 4 hours to caramelize onions. Use quick release to remove lid and stir occasionally.

When timer goes off, release lid and remove onions and set aside.
2. Wipe out the inner pot and set cooker to sauté. Add butter to melt and when melted, add celery and potatoes and cook, stirring occasionally, 12 minutes. Add garlic and cook 2 more minutes.
3. Sprinkle flour over vegetables and stir to coat. Add 2 cups broth and cook, stirring constantly till it thickens into gravy. Turn off heat.
4. Add onions, remaining broth, and beer to the pot. Stir well and serve.

White Bean & Tomato Bisque

Easy to make soup that warms you up from the inside. Serve with toasted cheese sandwiches or a warm chunk of crusty bread.

Serves: 6
Time: 30 minutes
Ingredients:
- 6 cups vegetable stock
- 2 cups canned navy beans (rinsed and drained)
- 1 14-oz. can tomatoes (diced)
- 4 celery stalks, (peeled and chopped)
- 2 medium carrots (peeled and chopped)
- 1 large yellow onion (peeled and chopped fine)

- 4 cloves garlic (cut into fourths)
- 2 tablespoons olive oil
- 2 bay leaves
- ½ tablespoon lemon juice
- ½ teaspoon kosher salt, divided
- ¼ teaspoon dried thyme
- ¼ teaspoon dried rosemary
- Freshly ground black pepper

Method:
1. Peel and chop all the vegetables; set aside.
2. Set your Instant Pot to Sauté and keep the temperature at normal. Add olive oil and heat until hot. Add onion and cook until golden brown, stirring frequently.
3. Add carrots, celery, and garlic and cook until almost tender, about 3 minutes, stirring occasionally.
4. Add remaining ingredients, except for lemon juice, and stir to combine. Cook on high pressure for 8-10 minutes.
5. Release the pressure and discard bay leaves.
6. Pour into blender, or use an immersion blender, and puree soup to desired consistency. Stir in lemon juice and serve.

Wild Rice & Mushroom Soup

A creamy, hearty soup, perfect for cold winter nights. Wild rice and shitake mushrooms give it an almost beefy flavor, without any beef. This recipe makes a large batch of soup, so plenty of leftovers for another day!

Serves: 10

Time: 60 minutes

Ingredients:

- 6 cups water
- 4 cups vegetable broth
- 2 cups shiitake mushrooms, sliced
- 2 cups coconut milk
- 1 cup wild rice, uncooked
- 5 celery stalks, chopped
- 2 large carrots, peeled and chopped
- 1 small onion, chopped
- 4 cloves garlic, chopped fine
- ¼ cup soy sauce
- ¼ cup fresh parsley, chopped
- 1 ½ teaspoons poultry seasoning
- 1 ½ teaspoons garlic powder
- Salt and pepper to taste

Method:

1. Add all ingredients, except coconut milk and parsley, to cooker. Close and lock lid. Select manual function and set timer to 45 minutes.
2. When timer goes off, use natural release to remove the lid. Stir in milk and parsley and serve.

Desserts

Almond Filled Peaches

Plump, ripe peaches stuffed with a cookie crumble filling and braised in wine! Can you say more? Easy to make and sure to impress your guests. Serve topped with whipped cream or ice cream.

Serves: 4

Time: 20 minutes

Ingredients:
- 3 peaches, ripe but still firm
- 1 cup almond cookies, crumbled
- 1 cup red wine
- 4 tablespoons sugar
- 2 tablespoons butter, melted
- 2 tablespoons almonds
- 1 teaspoon lemon zest

Method:

1. Wash peaches and slice in half. Remove the pit and enlarge the cavity with a spoon or melon baller.
2. Place the cookies, almonds in food processor and pulse until they are crumbs. Mix in zest and butter. Fill the peaches and place in steamer basket.
3. Add red wine to the cooker and gently lower steamer basket into the pot. Close and lock the lid. Select manual function and set timer for 3 minutes.
4. When timer goes off, remove lid with quick release. Gently remove peaches, using tongs, and place on serving plates.
5. Set cooker to sauté and reduce the remaining wine until it resembles syrup. Drizzle over peaches and serve.

Amaretto Cheesecake

Cheesecake in the pressure cooker? Yes! You will find a couple of my favorite cheesecake recipes in this chapter. This is one of my favorites. I just love Amaretto, and this one reminds me of a cheesecake I had in San Francisco years ago.

Serves: 6
Time: 50 minutes
Ingredients:
For the crust:
- 1 cup graham cracker crumbs

- 2 teaspoons sugar
- 1 teaspoon butter

For the filling:
- 1 lb. ricotta cheese
- 3 large eggs, separated
- ½ cup sugar
- ¼ cup heavy cream
- 2 tablespoons Amaretto
- 2 teaspoons flour
- ½ teaspoon each orange and lemon zest
- ½ teaspoon vanilla

Method:
1. For crust: use butter to grease a 6-inch springform pan. Combine cracker crumbs and sugar together in a bowl. Sprinkle evenly over prepared pan.
2. For the filling: in a large mixing bowl, beat all ingredients, except egg whites, about 4 minutes, or until smooth.
3. In a separate bowl, beat egg whites until soft peaks form. Gently fold into cheese mixture. Pour into prepared pan. Cover with paper towel, then foil.
4. Pour 1 ½ cups of water into cooker and place a trivet on the bottom. Using a foil sling, lower cheesecake onto trivet. Close and lock lid. Select manual setting

and set timer for 40 minutes. When timer goes off, use natural release to remove the lid.
5. Carefully remove cheesecake from the pot. Remove the foil and paper towel. Let cool for one hour. Refrigerate overnight for the best flavor.

Banana Nut Pudding

Steamed pudding is one of the easiest desserts to make in your Instant Pot. This one is creamy and rich with bananas, pecans, and a hint of cinnamon. Enjoy!

Serves: 8
Time: 80 minutes
Ingredients:
- 2 very ripe bananas, peeled and mashed
- 1 cup corn syrup
- 2/3 cup butter, soft
- 3 large eggs, at room temperature
- ½ cup self-rising flour
- ½ cup sugar
- ¼ cup pecans, chopped
- 1 tsp ground cinnamon
- ½ tsp baking powder

Method:

1. Pour 1 ½ cups water into pot. Butter bottom of 8-cup steamer basket. Line with parchment paper. Place the steamer basket in the pot. Pour ½ the syrup in the bottom of the basket.
2. In a large bowl, beat butter and sugar until light. Add eggs, one at a time, beating after each. Beat in remaining syrup.
3. In a separate bowl, combine dry ingredients. Add 1/2 the dry ingredients and pecan to butter mixture, fold in gently. Add ½ the banana, and fold again. Repeat with remaining ingredients. Pour into basket. Close and lock lid.
4. Select steam setting and set timer for 90 minutes. When timer goes off, use natural release to remove the lid. Invert pudding onto serving plate. Cut into wedges to serve.

Black & Blue Berry Cobbler

This slow cooked cobbler makes the perfect dessert any time of year. If fresh berries are hard to find, or too expensive in winter, frozen berries can be used. Packed with black and blue berries, serve with whipped cream or topped with ice cream.

Serves: 8
Time: 2 hours 10 minutes

Ingredients:

For the batter:
- 1 cup flour
- ¼ cup milk
- 1 egg
- 2 tablespoons vegetable oil
- 2 tablespoons sugar
- 1 teaspoon baking powder
- ¼ teaspoon cinnamon

For the berry filling:
- 4 cups blackberries and blueberries, mixed
- 1 cup sugar
- ¼ cup flour

Method:
1. For the batter: in a large bowl combine dry ingredients. Stir in egg, milk, and oil until combined.
2. Spray inner pot of cooker with cooking spray.
3. For the filling: combine the flour and sugar in a large bowl. Add berries and stir gently to coat.
4. Spread the batter on the bottom of the pot and top with berries. Close and lock lid. Select slow cooker function and set timer to 2 hours. When timer goes off, remove lid with quick release. Invert cobbler onto serving plate and serve.

Brown Rice & Pumpkin Pudding

The Instant Pot is the perfect kitchen accessory to make a creamy, dreamy rice pudding like this healthy version made with brown rice and pumpkin. Perfect after dinner treat in the fall.

Serves: 4
Time: 55 minutes
Ingredients:
- 3 cups milk
- 2 ¼ cups water
- 1 cup brown rice
- ½ cup pumpkin
- ¼ cup brown sugar, packed
- 1 teaspoon vanilla
- 1 teaspoon cinnamon
- ½ teaspoon ginger
- ½ teaspoon salt
- ¼ teaspoon nutmeg

Method:
1. Place water and rice into the cooker. Close and lock lid. Select manual setting and set the timer for 20 minutes. When the timer goes off, use natural release to remove the lid.

2. Set the cooker to sauté. Add milk, sugar, salt, and spices and bring to boil. Simmer, uncovered 20 minutes, stirring occasionally.
3. Add pumpkin and vanilla, cook another 10 minutes. Remove inner pot and let pudding sit for about 15 minutes. Serve.

Butterscotch Apple Bread Pudding

Bread pudding is a popular dessert in the south. It's a great way to save money since most of the recipes call for stale bread. This one combines apples and cinnamon with warm butterscotch, delish! Since this recipe makes a large batch of pudding, it is ideal for potlucks and parties. Serve topped with a dollop of whipped cream.

Serves: 24
Time: 2 hours 20 minutes
Ingredients:
- 22 caramels, wrappers removed
- 12 cups of bread, cubed
- 5 cups milk
- 1 can apple pie filling
- 8 eggs, beaten
- 2 cups light cream
- 1 package butterscotch instant pudding
- 1 teaspoon ground cinnamon

Method:
1. Spray inner pot with cooking spray. Set cooker to sauté and add caramels and 1 cup milk. Cook, stirring frequently, until caramels are completely melted.
2. Add pie filling, cream, eggs, cinnamon, and another cup of milk; combine thoroughly. Stir in bread.
3. Close and lock lid. Select slow cooker function and set timer for 2 hours. When timer goes off, remove the lid with natural release. Let sit for 10 minutes.
4. Meanwhile, in a small pot, over medium heat, whisk pudding mix with remaining milk. Cook, stirring frequently, just until sauce is heated through. Serve pudding drizzled with 2 tablespoons of sauce.

Caramel Filled Brownies

Ooey, gooey, chocolate brownies cooked in your pressure cooker! These brownies are even more special because they have warm caramel in the center!

Serves: 6
Time: 35 minutes
Ingredients:
- 1 ½ cup water
- 1 cup sugar
- 5 tablespoons butter, soft
- 5-6 Rolo candies

- ¾ cup flour
- 2 eggs
- ¼ cup unsweetened cocoa powder
- 1 tablespoon walnuts, chopped
- 1 ½ teaspoons vanilla
- ¾ teaspoon baking powder

Method:

1. In a large mixing bowl, combine butter and eggs and beat well. Add dry ingredients and stir to thoroughly combine. Stir in nuts.
2. Spray a 6-inch springform pan with cooking spray. Line bottom of pan with parchment paper. Place caramel candies in the middle.
3. Pour batter, evenly, into pan. Top with foil.
4. Place a trivet in the bottom of cooker and add water. Use a foil sling to place pan on trivet. Close and lock lid. Select manual function and set timer for 35 minutes. When timer goes off, remove lid with natural release. Carefully remove pan from cooker and let cool 10 minutes. Invert onto serving plate and remove parchment.

Caribbean Bread Pudding

This pudding packs in all the flavors of the Caribbean—coconut, bananas and lime. This is a great summertime dessert.

Serves: 6

Time: 85 minutes

Ingredients:
- 3 cups stale bread, cubed
- 1 ½ cups water
- 1 cup sour cream
- 1 cup coconut, toasted
- 1 cup ripe banana, sliced
- 1 cup almond milk
- 3 large egg yolks
- ½ cup cane sugar
- zest of 1 lime
- 1 large egg
- 1 tablespoon turbinado sugar
- 1 teaspoon vanilla
- 1 pinch salt

Method:
1. In a large bowl, beat yolks, egg, and sour cream until smooth. Add sugar, milk, salt, vanilla, and zest and beat again. Stir in bread, coconut, and banana; let set 1 hour.

2. Butter a 4-cup soufflé dish. Pour pudding into dish. Cover with foil, leaving room for the pudding to expand.
3. Place a trivet in the bottom of cooker and add water. Use a foil sling to lower soufflé dish onto trivet. Close and lock lid. Select manual setting and set timer for 20 minutes. When timer goes off, use quick release to remove the lid.
4. Carefully remove soufflé dish. Sprinkle with turbinado sugar and broil just until sugar turns brown. Serve.

Chocolate Peanut Butter Cheesecake

Chocolate and peanut butter, what a great combination! This is one dessert you will want to make for special occasions or whenever you just want to indulge that sweet tooth!

Serves: 8-10
Time: 85 minutes
Ingredients:
For the cheesecake:
- 2 packages cream cheese, softened
- 1 ¼ cups chocolate graham cracker crumbs
- ¾ cup semi-sweet chocolate chips
- ¾ cup peanut butter chips
- ½ cup sugar
- 4 tablespoons butter, melted

- 2 eggs
- 2 tablespoons sour cream
- ¾ teaspoon vanilla

For the topping:
- ¼ cup semi-sweet chocolate chips
- ¼ cup peanut butter morsels

Method:
1. In a small bowl, mix graham crumbs with butter until moist; set aside.
2. In a large bowl, beat cream cheese and sugar until no lumps remain. Add sour cream and vanilla and beat to combine. Add eggs, one at a time, beating well after each.
3. Pour the crumb mixture into a 6-inch springform pan and pack onto bottom and halfway up sides.
4. Place chocolate and peanut butter chips into separate bowls, and microwave, separately, at 30 second intervals, stirring after each until thoroughly melted.
5. Divide cheesecake filling in half. To one half, add melted chocolate and stir thoroughly. Pour into crust. Add peanut butter to the other half, stir well, and pour over chocolate layer. Cover with foil.
6. Place a trivet on the bottom of the cooker and add 1- 1 ½ cups water. Use a foil sling to lower pan onto trivet,

making sure pan does not touch water. Close and lock lid. Select manual setting and set timer for 2 ½ hours.
7. When timer goes off, use quick release to remove lid. Carefully remove cheesecake and let cool 1 hour. Refrigerate 4 hours or overnight.
8. When ready to serve, prepare the topping: melt the chips in 2 separate bowls again. Pour melted chips into a plastic baggie and clip off corner. Squeeze over cheesecake, serve.

Cookies 'N Cream Cake

A pressure cooker cake using Oreos! Every kid's idea of the perfect dessert. And yes, you can bake a cake in the pressure cooker. The trick is to remove the inner pot and add ½ cup salt to the cooker, close and lock the lid and cook 5 minutes to heat it up. This helps the cake to cook evenly.

Serves: 4
Time: 40 minutes
Ingredients:
- 16-20 Oreo cookies, ground in food processor to powder
- ½ cup milk
- 4 tablespoons sugar
- 1 tablespoon butter, soft
- 1 teaspoon baking soda

- 1 teaspoon baking powder
- powdered sugar, for dusting

Method:
1. Butter a 6-inch springform pan and line with parchment paper.
2. In mixing bowl, combine all ingredients and mix thoroughly. Pour into pan.
3. Remove inner pot from the cooker and add ½ cup salt. Close and lock lid. Set to manual setting and set timer for 5 minutes. When timer goes off, remove lid with quick release.
4. Use a foil sling to lower pan into cooker. Close and lock lid. Select manual setting and set timer for 20 minutes. When timer goes off, use natural release to remove lid. Do the toothpick test; if cake is not cooked through, cook 5 minutes more.
5. Remove pan from cooker and let cool completely. Remove sides of pan and dust top of cake with powdered sugar; serve.

Cranberry Apple Compote

This dessert is almost too easy to make! The combination of apples, raisins, and cranberries makes it the ideal treat for fall.

Serve over ice cream or topped with whipped cream.

Serves: 8

Time: 80 minutes

Ingredients:

- 1 can apple pie filling
- 1 can whole cranberry sauce
- ½ cup raisins
- 1 ½ tablespoons cinnamon
- ¼ teaspoon ground nutmeg

Method:

1. Spray inner pot with cooking spray.
2. Pour pie filling into large bowl and cut apples into smaller pieces. Add remaining ingredients and stir well.
3. Pour into cooker. Close and lock lid. Select slow cooker function and set timer for 90 minutes. When timer goes off, remove lid with quick release. Serve.

French Cherry Pie

This "pie" is based on the crustless French dessert called a clafoutis. The dessert uses fruit covered with a flan-like custard and is baked to perfection. You can substitute almost any fruit for the cherries.

Serves: 4

Time: 10 minutes

Ingredients:

- 2 cups cherries, pitted
- ¾ cup sour cream

- ½ cup flour
- 4 large egg yolks, room temperature
- 1/3 cup honey
- ¼ cup milk
- 1 tablespoon vanilla

Method:
1. Butter a 2-quart baking dish. Place trivet in bottom of cooker and add 2 cups water.
2. Add cherries to prepared dish.
3. In large bowl, mix all ingredients, except flour, thoroughly. Stir in flour until dissolved. Pour over cherries.
4. Use a foil sling to place dish on trivet. Close and lock lid. Select manual setting and set timer for 20 minutes. When timer goes off, remove lid with quick release. Remove dish from cooker and let cool 10 minutes. Serve warm.

Glossy Orange Steamed Pudding

This glossy pudding is truly a dessert meant for a special occasion. Caramelized orange slices decorate the top of the rich steamed pudding. Best when served warm.

Serves: 6
Time: 2 hours 10 minutes
Ingredients:

- 1 2/3 cups flour, sifted
- ½ cup butter, softened
- ½ cup superfine sugar
- 4 eggs
- 1/3 cup milk
- ½ lemon zest, finely grated
- 1 teaspoon vanilla extract

For the caramelized oranges:
- 2 oranges, peels on, sliced into thin rounds
- 2 cups superfine sugar
- 2 cups water

Method:
1. Pour 1 ½ cups water into pot. Butter bottom of 8-cup steamer basket. Line with parchment paper. Place the steamer basket in the pot.
2. In a large bowl, beat butter, sugar, and vanilla until pale and thick. Add eggs, one at a time, beating well after each. Fold in flour and zest. Fold in milk.
3. Pour into prepared steamer basket and top with layer of foil. Close and lock lid. Select steam setting and set timer for 90 minutes. When timer goes off, remove lid with natural release.
4. To caramelize oranges: place orange slices in medium pot and add just enough water to cover. Over medium

heat, bring to simmer, then drain. Repeat this process one more time.
5. Add blanched oranges to a saucepan with sugar and water. Over medium heat, bring to simmer, stirring occasionally to dissolve sugar. Cook for 10-12 minutes or until oranges are translucent. Remove from heat and let cool.
6. When the pudding is done, invert onto serving plate. Top with orange slices and drizzle syrup over top. Serve.

Green Tea Pudding

A healthy dessert with the caramelized sugar topping found on crème brulees. This is the perfect dessert for folks who don't enjoy overly sweet dishes, and no one needs to know it's good for them!

Serves: 8
Time: 40 minutes
Ingredients:
- 1 ½ cup cream
- 1 ½ cups water
- 1 cup coconut milk
- 6 extra large egg yolks
- 6 tablespoons sugar

- 1 tablespoon matcha green tea powder
- 1 ¼ teaspoon vanilla extract
- 1 pinch sea salt

For topping:
- 2 teaspoons sugar per ramekin

Method:
1. Set cooker to sauté. Add cream, milk, tea, vanilla, and salt and cook, stirring constantly till heated through.
2. In a medium bowl, whisk yolks and sugar till blended. Add cream mixture, a little at a time, whisking constantly. Continue until all the cream has been tempered into the eggs. Pour mixture through fine mesh sieve. Then pour into 8 ramekins. Wrap each ramekin tightly with foil.
3. Place trivet in cooker and add water. Place ramekins on trivet. Close and lock lid. Select manual setting and set timer for 12 minutes.
4. When timer goes off, remove lid with natural release. Carefully remove ramekins and let cool. Refrigerate 4 hours or overnight.
5. To serve: remove foil and sprinkle the tops of each with sugar. Use a blow torch, if you have one, to melt and caramelize sugar, or you can place under broiler until sugar melts and caramelizes. Serve.

Lemonade Pie

This light, refreshing pie is the perfect summertime dessert. Easy to make and fun to eat. A great pie to make for pool parties and backyard BBQs!

Serves: 6-8

Time: 50 minutes

Ingredients:

For the crust:
- ¾ cup graham cracker crumbs
- 3 tablespoons butter, melted
- 1 tablespoon sugar

For the filling:
- 4 large egg yolks
- 1 can sweetened condensed milk
- ½ cup fresh lemon juice
- 1/3 cup sour cream
- 2 tablespoons lemon zest, grated

Method:

1. Spray a 7-inch springform pan with cooking spray.
2. In a small bowl, combine all crust ingredients. Press evenly on bottom and sides of pan. Freeze 10 minutes.
3. For the filling: in a large bowl, beat egg yolks until pale. Gradually beat in condensed milk until mixture thickens. Gradually beat in lemon juice until smooth.

Stir in sour cream and zest. Pour into crust. Cover top with foil.
4. Place a trivet on bottom of cooker and add 1 cup water. Use a foil sling to lower pan onto trivet. Close and lock lid. Select manual setting and set timer for 15 minutes. When timer goes off, remove lid with natural release. Check to make sure middle is set; if not, cook 5 more minutes.
5. Remove pan from cooker to cool. When cooled, cover with plastic wrap and refrigerate 4 hours or overnight. Top with whip cream and serve.

Pina Colada Rice Pudding

A creamy rice pudding that tastes like a tropical cocktail! This pudding is a tasty summertime treat everyone will love. Serve garnished with sliced pineapple and toasted coconut.

Serves: 6
Time: 25 minutes
Ingredients:
- 2 ½ cups water
- 2 cups white rice, uncooked
- 1 large can crushed pineapple, drained
- 1 cup heavy cream
- ¼ cup coconut
- ¼ cup sugar

- ½ teaspoon vanilla

Method:
1. Add water and rice to cooker. Close and lock lid. Select manual setting and set timer to 20 minutes. When timer goes off, remove lid with natural release. Transfer rice to a bowl and let cool. Cover with plastic wrap and refrigerate up to 2 hours.
2. In a large bowl, beat cream, sugar, and vanilla until stiff peaks form, about 3 minutes. Gently fold in rice, pineapple, and coconut. Cover with plastic wrap and refrigerate 3 hours or overnight. Serve.

Pineapple Carrot Cake

One of my all-time favorite desserts! The pineapple in this recipe creates a cake that is super moist. I usually make this recipe with the walnuts added to the cake and omit the raisins, but you can make it however your family likes it!

Serves: 10-12

Time: 90 minutes

Ingredients:
- 2 cups flour
- 3 carrots, peeled and grated
- 1 ¼ cups brown sugar, packed
- 1 cup crushed pineapple, drained
- ½ cup vegetable oil

- ½ cup raisins
- 2 eggs
- ¼ cup water
- 2 teaspoons cinnamon
- 2 teaspoons baking powder
- 1 teaspoon baking soda
- 1 teaspoon vanilla
- ½ teaspoon nutmeg
- ½ teaspoon salt

For the topping:
- 1 cup heavy cream
- 3 tablespoons sugar
- ¼ cup walnuts, chopped

Method:
1. Spray the inner pot with cooking spray.
2. In a large bowl, beat brown sugar, eggs, oil, water, and vanilla until smooth.
3. Add flour, baking powder, baking soda, cinnamon, nutmeg, and salt and stir to combine. Add carrots, pineapple, and raisins and stir until moistened.
4. Pour batter into pot. Close and lock lid. Select slow cooker function and set timer for 2 hours or until cake passes the toothpick test. When timer goes off, remove the lid with natural release.
5. Invert cake onto serving plate and let cool.

6. For topping: Beat cream and sugar together until soft peaks form. When cake has cooled completely, spread with topping and garnish with chopped nuts.

Salted Caramel Apple Dip

All the flavor of the all-American apple pie in a fun-to-eat dip. This is one way to get the kids to eat more fruit!

Serves: 8

Time: 20 minutes

Ingredients:

- 5 cups Granny Smith apples, peeled, cored, and diced
- 1 jar caramel ice cream topping
- 1 pkg. refrigerated pie crusts
- 1/8 cup milk
- 2 tablespoons sugar
- 1 teaspoon cinnamon, divided
- Pinch of sea salt and nutmeg

Method:

1. Heat oven to 350 degrees.
2. In a small bowl, combine sugar with remaining cinnamon. Lay one pie crust on a baking sheet and brush with milk. Sprinkle half the sugar mixture over the crust. Cut into strips and bake till golden brown, about 10 minutes. Repeat with other pie crust.

3. Spray the inner pot with cooking spray. Add apples, caramel, ½ the cinnamon along with the salt and nutmeg. Stir to combine.
4. Add lid and lock in place. Set for manual and timer for 2 minutes.
5. Pour dip into serving bowl and serve with pie crust dippers.

Mocha Café Steamed Pudding

This steamed pudding combines two of the best flavors, chocolate and coffee! Like an expensive coffee house drink but in a tasty dessert. This recipe is made in coffee cups, but you can use a bowl that is oven proof, too.

Serves: 4

Time: 20 mins

Ingredients:
- 1 ¼ cups self-rising flour
- 1 cup heavy cream
- 2/3 cup cocoa powder
- 2/3 cup brown sugar
- 1/3 cup milk, warmed
- 4 tablespoons butter, softened
- 2 large eggs
- 1 tablespoon instant coffee

- 1 teaspoon vanilla bean paste
- 1 packet hot cocoa mix, for garnish

Method:
1. Lightly butter 4 coffee cups.
2. In a small bowl, dissolve coffee in milk.
3. In a large bowl, beat butter and sugar until smooth. Add eggs, one at a time, beating after each. Sift in flour and cocoa powder, fold in until the batter is smooth. Spoon into prepared cups.
4. Pour 1 cup water into inner pot and place steaming shelf inside. Place cups on the shelf and close and lock lid. Select steam function and set timer for 15 minutes. When timer goes off, use quick release to remove lid. Remove pudding cups and let sit for 5 minutes.
5. Before serving, dust tops of pudding with hot cocoa mix.

Whiskey Pumpkin Cheesecake

This rich dessert combines everyone's favorite fall flavor, pumpkin, with bourbon! The texture of this cheesecake is smooth and somewhat firmer than pumpkin pie, but not as dense as cheesecake. Start a new tradition and serve this for the holidays instead of the usual pumpkin pie!

Serves: 8-10

Time: 55 minutes

Ingredients:
For the crust:
- ¾ cup graham cracker crumbs
- ¼ cup pecans, chopped fine
- 1/8 cup brown sugar, packed
- 1/8 cup sugar
- 2 tablespoons butter, melted
- ¼ teaspoon ginger

For the filling:
- 1 block cream cheese, softened
- ¾ cup pumpkin, pureed
- ¼ cup sugar
- ¼ cup brown sugar, packed
- ¼ cup heavy cream
- 2 large eggs, room temperature
- 1 egg yolk, room temperature
- 1 ½ tablespoons bourbon
- 1 tablespoon cornstarch
- 1 ½ teaspoons cinnamon
- ½ teaspoon sea salt
- ½ teaspoon vanilla
- ¼ teaspoon nutmeg
- ¼ teaspoon ginger

For the topping:
- 1 cup sour cream

- ½ tablespoon bourbon
- 1 tablespoon sugar

Method:

1. For the crust: add graham crumbs, sugar, and pecans to food processor. Pulse until small crumbs form. Add melted butter and pulse until combined.
2. Butter a 6-inch springform pan. Press crust mixture firmly on bottom and 1 inch up sides of buttered pan. Freeze 15 minutes.
3. For the filling: in a large bowl, beat cream cheese, sugars, pumpkin, cornstarch, spices, salt, bourbon, and vanilla until smooth.
4. Add eggs and yolk, one at a time, beating after each just until combined. Stir in the cream. Pour into crust. Cover top with paper towel then foil, leaving room for cheesecake to expand.
5. Pour 1 ½ cups water into cooker and add trivet. Use a foil sling to lower cheesecake onto trivet. Close and lock lid. Select manual setting and set timer for 40 minutes. When timer goes off, use natural release to remove lid.
6. Carefully remove cheesecake. Remove foil and paper towel and let cool 1 hour. Cover and refrigerate 4 hours or overnight.

7. For the topping: in a medium bowl, beat ingredients together. Before serving, remove side of pan and spread with topping

White Chocolate Raspberry Bread Pudding

White chocolate and raspberries combine to make this your go-to bread pudding. If fresh raspberries are not in season, you can use frozen, just be sure to thaw and drain them thoroughly. Serve topped with a dollop of whip cream if you like.

Serves: 8
Time: 1 hour 40 minutes
Ingredients:
- 6 cups French bread, cubed
- 4 eggs
- 1 bar of white chocolate for baking, chopped
- 1 can sweetened condensed milk
- 1 cup fresh raspberries, rinsed and drained
- ¾ cup warm water
- 1 teaspoon vanilla

Method:
1. Spray inner pot with cooking spray. Add bread and sprinkle with white chocolate.

2. In a medium bowl, beat remaining ingredients, except berries, till thoroughly combined. Pour over bread.
3. Close and lock lid. Select slow cooker function and set timer for 90 minutes. When timer goes off, use natural release to remove lid. Check for doneness, if it does not pass the toothpick test, replace lid and cook another 15-20 minutes. Let cool 10-15 minutes.
4. Invert onto serving plate and garnish with fresh raspberries. Serve warm

Made in the USA
San Bernardino, CA
30 April 2018